BIBLE CH

By

D. L. MOODY

Chicago : New York : Toronto
Fleming H. Revell Company
Publishers of Evangelical Literature

1888

Inspiring and uplifting classics from authors such as:

E. M. Bounds
Amy Carmichael
Alfred Edersheim
Jonathan Edwards
Charles Finney
D. L. Moody
G. Campbell Morgan
George Muller
Andrew Murray
Charles Spurgeon
Hudson Taylor
R. A. Torrey
John Wesley
…and many more!

"Great Classics at Great Prices!"
www.ClassicChristianBooks.com

TABLE OF CONTENTS:

Preface 4

Chapter 1: The Captives In Babylon 5

Chapter 2: Thou Art The Head Of Gold! 9

Chapter 3: Nebuchadnezzars Image. 13

Chapter 4: Nebuchadnezzars Second Dream 20

Chapter 5: The Handwriting On The Wall. 24

Chapter 6: The Edict Of Darius. 27

Chapter 7: The Den Of Lions. 34

Chapter 8: Enoch 40

Chapter 9: Lot 49

Chapter 10: Jacob 58

Chapter 11: John The Baptist 68

PREFACE

THE STUDY OF the men and women of the Bible has been to me one of the most intense interest. The ways of God with different men, in different periods, and under different circumstances, yet always revealing the same wisdom, love and power, have filled me with wonder and with praise. I send forth the few sketches contained in the following pages in the hope that others may be led to similar studies with as much instruction and delight as these have afforded me.

D. L. Moody.

CHAPTER 1: THE CAPTIVES IN BABYLON

"But Daniel purposed in his heart that he would not defile himself with the portion of the king's meat, nor with the wine which he drank: therefore he requested of the prince of the eunuchs that he might not defile himself" (Daniel 1:8)

I ALWAYS DELIGHT to study the life of Daniel the Prophet. The name Daniel means God is my judge. God is my judge: not the public is my judge; not my fellow men, but God. So Daniel held himself responsible to God. Some may ask, Who was Daniel? Listen. About six hundred years before the time of Christ, the sins of the kings of Judah had brought down upon them and upon the people the judgments of God. Jehoiakim had succeeded Jehoahaz; and Jehoiachin had succeeded Jehoiakim; and he again was succeeded by Zedekiah; and of each of these kings the record runs just the same: "he did evil in the sight of the Lord."

No wonder that in the days of Jehoiakim, about six hundred years before the time of Christ, Nebuchadnezzar, King of Babylon, was permitted of God to come up against Jerusalem, and to lay siege against it and overcome it. It was probably at this time that Daniel, with some of the young princes, was carried away captive. A few years later, Jehoiachin being king, Nebuchadnezzar again came up against Jerusalem, and overcame it; when he bare away many of the temple vessels, and made several thousand captives.

And still later on, when Zedekiah was king, Nebuchadnezzar came a third time against Jerusalem to besiege it; and this time he burnt the city with fire; broke down its walls; slaughtered many of the people; and probably bore away another batch of captives to the banks of the Euphrates.

Among the earlier captives taken by the King of Babylon in the days of Jehoiakim, were four young men. Like Timothy in later times, they may have had godly mothers, who taught them the law of the Lord. Or they may perhaps have been touched by the words of Jeremiah, the weeping prophet, whom God had sent to the people of Judah. So, when the nation was rejecting the God of Israel, the God of Abraham, of Isaac, and of Moses, these young men took Him as their God: they received Him into their hearts.

Many may have mocked at Jeremiah's warnings, when he lifted up his voice against the sins of the people; they may have laughed at his tears, and have told him to his face - just as people say nowadays of earnest preachers - that he was causing undue excitement. But these four young men would seem to have listened to the prophets voice; and they had the strength to come out for God. And now they are in Babylon. Nebuchadnezzar the king commands that a certain number of the most promising of the young Jewish captives should be picked out, who might be taught the Chaldean tongue and instructed in the learning of Babylon. And the king further ordered that there should be daily set before them portions of meat from his table, and a supply of the same wine as he himself drank; and this was to go on for three years. And at the end of three years these young men were to stand before the great monarch, at that time the ruler over the whole world. Daniel and his three young friends were amongst those thus selected.

No young man ever goes from a country home to a large city - say, to a great metropolis - without grave temptations crossing his path on his entrance. And just at this turning point in his life, as in Daniel's, must lie the secret of his success or his failure. The cause of many of the failures that we see in life is, that men do not start right. Now, this young man started right. He took a character with him up to Babylon; and he was not ashamed of the religion of his mother and his father. He was not ashamed of the God of the Bible. Up there among those heathen idolaters he was not ashamed to let his light shine. The young Hebrew captive took his stand for God as he entered the gate of Babylon, and doubtless he cried to God to keep him steadfast. And he needed to cry hard, for he had to face great difficulties: as we shall see.

Soon comes a testing time. The king's edict goes forth, that these young men should eat the meat from the king's table. Some of that food would in all probability consist of meats prohibited by the Levitical law - the flesh of animals, of birds, and of fishes, which had been pronounced unclean, and were consequently forbidden: or in the preparation, some portion might not perhaps have been thoroughly drained of the blood, concerning which it had been declared, "Ye shall eat the blood of no manner of flesh;" or some part of the food may have been presented as an offering to Bel or some other Babylonish god. Some one of these circumstances, or possibly all of them united, may have determined Daniel's course of action. I do not think it took young Daniel long to make up his mind. "He purposed in his heart" - IN HIS HEART, mark that! - "that he would not defile himself with the portion of the king's meat."

If some modern Christians could have advised Daniel, they would have said, "Do not act like that; do not set aside the king's meat: that is an act of Pharisaism. The moment you take your stand, and say you will not eat it, you say in effect that you are better than other people." Oh, yes; that is the kind of talk too often heard now. Men say, "When you are in Rome you must do as Rome does;" and such people would have pressed upon the poor young captive that, though he might obey the commandments of God while in his own country, yet that he could not possibly do so here in Babylon - that he could not expect to carry his religion with him into the land of his captivity. I can imagine men saying to Daniel, "Look here, young man, you are too puritanical. Don't be too particular; don't have too many religious scruples. Bear in mind you are not now in Jerusalem. You will have to get over these notions, now you are here in Babylon. You are not now surrounded by friends and relatives. You are not a Jerusalem prince now. You are not surrounded by the royal family of Judah. You have been brought down from your high position. You are now a captive. And if the monarch hears about your refusing to eat the same kind of meat that he eats, and to drink the same kind of wine that he drinks, your head will soon roll from off your shoulders. You had better be a little politic."

But this young man had piety and religion deep down in his heart: and that is the right place for it; that is where it will grow; that is where it will have power; that is where it will regulate the life. Daniel had not joined the company of the church, the faithful few in Jerusalem - because he wanted to get into society, and attain a position: that was not the reason. It was because of the love he had toward the Lord God of Israel.

I can imagine the astonishment of that officer, Melzar, when Daniel told him could not eat the king's meat or drink his wine. "Why, what do you mean? Is there anything wrong with it? Why, it is the best the land can produce!"

"No," says Daniel, "there is nothing wrong with it in that way; but take it away, I cannot eat it." Then Melzar tried to reason Daniel out of his scruples; but no, there stood the prophet, youth though he was at that time, firm as a rock. So, thank God, this young Hebrew and his three friends said they would not eat the meat or drink the wine; and requesting that the portions might be taken away, they endeavored to persuade the overseer to bring them pulse instead.

"Take away this wine, and take away this meat. Give us pulse and water. "The prince of the eunuchs probably trembled for the consequences. But, yielding to their importunity, he eventually consented to let them have pulse and water for ten days. And lo! at the end of the ten days his fears were dispelled; for the faces of Daniel and his young friends were fairer and fatter than the faces of any of those who had partaken of the king's meat. The four young men had not noses, like those of too many men nowadays seen in our streets, as red as if they were just going to blossom. It is God's truth - and Daniel and his friends tested it - that cold water, with a clear conscience, is better than wine. They had a clear conscience; and the smile of God was upon them. The Lord had blessed their obedience, and the four Hebrew youths were allowed to have their own way; and in God's time they were brought into favor, not only with the officer set over them, but with the court and the king.

Daniel thought more of his principles than he did of earthly honor, or the esteem of men. Right was right with him. He was going to do right TODAY, and let the morrows take care of themselves. That firmness of purpose, in the strength of God, was the secret of his success. Right there, that very moment, he overcame. And from that hour, from that moment, he could go on conquering and to conquer, because he had started right.

Many a man is lost because he does not start right. He makes a bad start. A young man comes from his country home, and enters upon city life: temptation arises, and he becomes false to his principles. He meets with some scoffing, sneering man, who jeers at him because he goes to a church service; or because he is seen reading his Bible; or because he is known to pray to God - to that God to whom Daniel prayed in Babylon. And the young man proves to be weak-kneed: he cannot stand the scoffs, and the sneers, and the jeers, of his companions; and so he becomes untrue to his principles, and gives them up.

I want to say here to young men, that when a young man makes a wrong start, in ninety-nine cases out of a hundred it is ruin to him. The first game of chance; the first betting transaction; the first false entry in the books; the first quarter dollar taken from the cash-box or the till; the first night spent in evil company - either of these may prove the turning-point; either of these may represent a wrong start.

If ever any persons could be said to have had a good excuse for being unfaithful to their principles, these four young men might. They had been torn away from the associations of their childhood and their youth; had been taken away from the religious influences which centered in Jerusalem, away from the temple services and sacrifices; and had been put down in Babylon among the idols and idolaters, among the wise men and soothsayers, and the whole nation was against them. They went right against the current of the whole world.

BUT GOD WAS WITH THEM.

And when a man, for the sake of principle and conscience, goes against the current of the whole world, God is with him; and he need not stop to consider what the consequences will be. Right is right.

But our testimony for God is not limited to a single act: it has to last all through our lives. So we must not imagine for a moment that Daniel had only one trial to undergo. The word to the Lord's servants is the same in all ages, "Be thou faithful unto death."

This city of Babylon was a vast place. I suppose it to have been the largest city the world has ever seen. It is said to have been sixty miles round, and is understood to have consisted of an area of two hundred square miles. A line drawn through the city in either direction would measure fifteen miles. The walls are said to have had an elevation of three hundred and fifty feet: they would therefore be nearly on a level with the dome of St. Paul's Cathedral. The breadth of the walls is said to have been over eighty feet, and on the top eight chariots could run abreast. Babylon was like Chicago - so flat, that for ornamentation men had to construct artificial mounds; and, like Chicago in another particular, the products of vast regions flowed right into and through it.

CHAPTER 2: THOU ART THE HEAD OF GOLD!

"Nebuchadnezzar dreamed dreams, wherewith his spirit was troubled, and his sleep brake from him" (Daniel 2:1).

WE HEAR OF Daniel again some few years later on, and under new conditions. The King of Babylon had a dream; and his dream greatly disturbed him. He musters before him the magicians, the astrologers, the soothsayers, and the Chaldeans (or learned men), and requires from them the interpretation of this night-vision of his. He either cannot or will not narrate to them the incidents of the vision, but demands an explanation without detailing what he had seen in his dream:

"The thing is gone from me: if ye will not make known unto me the dream, with the interpretation thereof, ye shall be cut in pieces and your houses shall be made a dunghill."

That was a pretty unreasonable demand. It is true that he offered them rewards and honors if they succeeded. But of course they failed. And they admitted their failure. "There is not a man upon the earth that can show the king's matter: therefore there is no king, Lord, nor ruler that asked such things of any magician, astrologer, or Chaldean. And it is a rare thing that the king requireth; and there is none other that can show it before the king, except the gods, whose dwelling is not with men."

"Except the gods." They did not mean the God of Heaven - Daniel's God. He could have revealed the secret quick enough. They meant the idol-gods of Babylon, with whom these so-called wise men thought, and wrongly thought, the power of interpretation lay.

"There is not a man upon the earth that can show the king's matter". They were wrong there; and that they soon found out. "The king was angry and very furious, and commanded to destroy all the wise men of Babylon; and the decree went forth that the wise men should be slain; and they sought Daniel and his fellows to be slain."

The king's officer came to Daniel; but Daniel was not afraid. Says the officer to him, "You are classed among the wise men; and our orders are to take you out and execute you." "Well," says the young Hebrew captive, "the king has been very hasty. But let him only give me a little time; and I will show the interpretation."

He had read the law of Moses; and he was one of those who believed that what Moses had written concerning secret things was true: "The secret things belong unto the Lord our God; but the things that are revealed belong unto us, and to our children." He probably said to himself, My God knows that secret; and I will trust to Him to reveal it to me. And he may have called together his three friends; and have held a prayer meeting - perhaps the first prayer meeting ever held in Babylon. They dealt with the threatening message of the King of Babylon just as Hezekiah had dealt with the threatening letter of the King of Assyria a hundred years before. They spread it before the Lord. And they prayed that this secret might be revealed to them. And after they had prayed, and made their request to God - and the answer did not come right off, then and there - they went off to bed, and fell asleep. I do not think that you or I would have slept much, if we had thought that our heads were in danger of coming off in the morning. Daniel slept: for we are told the matter was revealed to him in a dream or night-vision. Daniel's faith was strong: so he could sleep calmly in the prospect of death. If his friends did not sleep through the night it is most likely they were praying.

DANIEL STANDS BEFORE THE KING.

In the morning Daniel pours out his heart in thanksgiving. He blessed the God of Heaven. He had got into the spirit of Psalm 103: "Bless the Lord, O my soul, and all that is within me, bless His holy name!" Paul and Silas had the same spirit of thanksgiving when they were in the prison at Philippi. Daniel makes his way to the palace, goes into the guard-room, and says to the officer: Bring me in before the king; and I will show unto the king the interpretation. He stands in the presence of Nebuchadnezzar; and, like Joseph before Pharaoh, before proceeding to unfold the dream, he gives glory to God: There is a God in Heaven that revealeth secrets. Daniel took his place as nobody: he himself was nothing. He did not wish the king to think highly of him. That is the very highest type of piety - when a man hides himself, as it were, out of the way; and seeks to exalt his God and lift up his Redeemer, and not himself. And then he proceeds to describe the dream: "Thou, O king, sawest; and behold, a great image! This great image, whose brightness was excellent, stood before thee; and the form thereof was terrible."

I can imagine how the king's eyes flashed out at those opening words; and I can fancy him crying out, "Yes, that is it: the whole thing comes back to me now."

"This images head was of fine gold; his breast and his arms of silver; his belly and his thighs of brass; his legs of iron; his feet, part of iron and part of clay."

"Yes, that is it exactly," says the king; "I recollect all that now. But surely there was something more."

And Daniel goes on: "Thou sawest till that a stone was cut out without hands, which smote the image upon his feet that were of iron and clay, and brake them to pieces.... This is the dream: and we will tell the interpretation thereof before the king."

And then, amidst death-like stillness, Daniel went on to unfold the interpretation; and he told the king that the golden head of the great image was none other than himself. "Thou art this head of gold!" He then goes on to tell of another kingdom that should arise - not so beautiful, but stronger; as silver is stronger than gold: that described the Medo-Persian empire. But the arms of silver were to overthrow the head of gold. And Daniel himself lived to see the day when that part of the prophetic dream came to pass. He lived to see Cyrus overthrow the Chaldean power. He lived to see the scepter of empire pass into the hands of the Medes and Persians. And after them came a mighty Grecian conqueror, Alexander the Great, who overthrew the Persian dynasty; and for awhile Greece ruled the world. Then came the Caesars, and founded the empire of Rome - symbolized by the legs of iron - the mightiest power the world had ever known: and for centuries Rome sat on those seven hills, and swayed the scepter over the nations of the earth. And then, in its turn, the Roman power was broken; and the mighty empire split up into ten kingdoms corresponding to the ten toes of the prophetic figure.

I believe in the literal fulfillment, so far, of Daniel's God-given words; and in the sure fulfillment of the final prophecy of the stone cut out of the mountain, without hands, that by and by shall grind the kingdoms of this world into dust, and bring in the kingdom of peace.

Whilst the feet were of clay, there was some of the strength of the iron remaining in them. At the present day we have got down to the toes, and even to the extremities of these. Soon, very soon, the collision may occur; and then will come the end. The stone cut out without hands is surely coming - and it may be very soon.

What does Ezekiel say, prophesying within some few years of the time of this very vision? "Remove the diadem, and take off the crown...I will overturn, overturn, overturn; and it shall be no more, until He come whose right it is: and I will give it Him."

What does Paul say? "The appearing of our Lord Jesus Christ; which in His time He shall show, who is the blessed and only Potentate; the King of kings; and Lord of lords;.... to whom be honor and power everlasting."

Yes, the Fifth Monarchy is coming: and it may be very soon. Hail, thou Fifth Monarch, who art to rule the world in righteousness, and sway the scepter from the river unto the ends of the earth. Shortly the cry, Christ is come! will be ringing through the earth. It is only a little while. Cheer up, ye children of God; our King will be back by and by! And to those who have not as yet given their hearts to Christ, I would say, Lose no time! If you want a part and lot in that coming kingdom of the Lord you had better press into it now while the door is open. By and by Too late! too late! will be the cry.

When King Nebuchadnezzar heard the full description of his dream and listened to its interpretation, he was satisfied that at last he had found a really wise man. He gave Daniel many great gifts, and raised him - just as Pharaoh had raised Joseph ages before - to a place near the throne. And when Daniel was raised to position and power he did not forget his friends; he requested of the king that they should be promoted; and they also were put in positions of honor and trust. God blessed them signally; and - what is more - He kept them true to Him in their prosperity, as they had been in their adversity.

From that moment Daniel becomes a great man. He is set over the province of Babylon: he is lifted right out of bondage; right out of servitude. He was a young man, probably not more than twenty-two years old: and there he is - set over a mighty empire; is made, you might say, practically ruler over the whole of the then known world. And God will exalt us when the right time comes. We need not try to promote ourselves; we need not struggle for position. Let God put us in our true places. And it is a good deal better for a man to be right with God, even if he hold no position down here. Then he can look up and know that God is pleased with him: that is enough.

"FIGHT THE GOOD FIGHT!"

How goes the fight with thee
The life-long battle with all evil things?
Thine no low strife, and thine no selfish aim;
It is the war of giants and of kings.
Goes the fight well with thee
This living fight with death and deaths dark power?
Is not the Stronger than the strong one near,
With thee and for thee in the fiercest hour?
Dread not the din and smoke,
The stifling poison of the fiery air;
Courage! it is the battle of thy God:
Go, and for Him learn how to do and dare!
What though ten thousand fall,
And the red field with the dear dead be strewn!
Grasp but more bravely thy bright shield and sword;
Fight to the last, although thou fightest alone.
What though ten thousand faint,
Desert, or yield, or in weak terror flee?
Heed not the panic of the multitude;
Thine be the Captain's watchword - Victory!

- Dr. H. Bonar

CHAPTER 3: NEBUCHADNEZZARS IMAGE.

"Nebuchadnezzar the king made an image of gold, whose height was three-score cubits: he set it up in the plains of Dur in the province of Babylon" (Daniel 3:1)

TIME WENT ON - possibly several years; and now we reach a crisis indeed. Whether or not that dream of a gigantic human figure continued to haunt Nebuchadnezzar we cannot say; but it is quite possible that the dream may have in some sort suggested Nebuchadnezzar's next proceeding. He ordered the construction of an immense image. It was to be of gold - not simply gilded, but actually of gold. Gold is a symbol of prosperity; and at this time Babylon was prosperous. In like manner in the prosperous days of Jerusalem, gold was abundant. And it may have been that some of the precious metal, carried as the spoils of war from the Jewish capital, was used in the construction of this image of gold. It was of colossal size - over ninety feet high, and between nine and ten feet wide. This gigantic image was set up in the plain of Dura, near to the city. I suppose Nebuchadnezzar wanted to gratify his imperial vanity by inaugurating a universal religion.

When the time came for the dedication, Daniel was not there. He may have been away in Egypt; or in some one of the many provinces, attending to the affairs of the empire. If he had been there we should have heard of him. Satraps, princes, governors, counselors, high secretaries, judges, were ordered to be present at the dedication of the image. What a gathering that morning! It was the fashionable thing to be seen that morning driving to the plain of Dura. Of course it was: all the great people, and all the rich people, were to be there. Now hark! the trumpet sounds; the herald shouts: "To you it is commanded, O people, nations, and languages, that at what time ye hear the sound of the cornet, flute, harp, sackbut, psaltery, dulcimer, and all kinds of music, ye fall down and worship the golden image that Nebuchadnezzar the king hath set up: and whoso falleth not down and worshippeth, shall the same hour be cast into the midst of a burning fiery furnace."

Perhaps a part of the ceremony consisted in the unveiling of the statue, as we say. One thing, however, is certain: that at the given signal all the people were required to fall to the earth, and worship. But in the law of God there was something against that: God's voice had spoken at Sinai; God's finger had written on the table of stone – "Thou Shalt Have None Other gods before Me." God's law went right against the kings. I said Daniel was not on the plain of Dura. But his influence was there. He had influenced those three friends of his - Shadrach, Meshach, and Abednego. They were there; and they were actuated by the same spirit as Daniel. Their position brought them here at the hour of the dedication.

Now mark you, no man can be true for God, and live for Him, without at some time or other being unpopular in this world. Those men who are trying to live for both worlds make a wreck of it; for at some time or other the collision is sure to come. Ah, would all of us have advised Daniel's three friends to do the right thing at any hazard? Are there not some of us with so little backbone that we would have counseled these three just to bow down a little, so that no one could take notice - to merely bow down, but not to worship? Daniel and his friends, when they first came to Babylon, perceived that the two worlds - the present world and the world to come - would be in collision: and they went for the world to come; they went for things unseen: they did not judge for the time being only; they took their stand right there. Even if it cost them their lives, what of that! It would only hasten them to the glory; and they would receive the greater reward. They took their stand for God and for the unseen world. The faithful three utterly refused to bend the knee to a God of gold. A terrible penalty was associated with disobedience to the king's command: "Whoso falleth not down and worshippeth shall the same hour be cast into the midst of a burning fiery furnace."

How many would cry out in this city - in every city - Give me gold, give me money; and I will do anything. Some people may think and say that the men of Nebuchadnezzar's day ought not to have bowed down to a golden idol; but they themselves are every day doing just that very thing. Money is their God; social position their golden image. There are plenty of men today who are bowing down to the golden image that the world has set up. "Give me gold! give me gold; and you may have Heaven. Give me position; and you may have the world to come. Give me worldly honor; and I will sell out my hopes of Heaven. Give me the thirty pieces of silver; and I will give you Christ." That is the cry of the world today.

And now the order is given - very probably by the king himself - that the bands should strike up; just the same as on public occasions bands of music do now. The music could be heard afar off; and when the first notes burst forth all were to bow down to the golden image. Earth's great ones and mighty ones bowed down at the king's command. But there were three with stiff knees which did not bend. Those were Daniel's three friends, who knew well that to do the king's bidding would be to break the law of their God; and they at all events will not fall down and worship. At the king's command they had come to the dedication: there might be nothing wrong in that: but they will not bow down. They were too stiff in the backbone for that. They remembered the command, "Thou shalt have none other gods before Me." These are the kind of servants God wants - men who will stand up bravely and fearlessly for Him.

Like all the servants of the Lord, and all who walk in the atmosphere of Heaven, these three Hebrews had enemies. There were some who bore them a bitter grudge. Very possibly they were thought to have had undue preference in being promoted to office. So there were some others, besides the three young

Hebrews, who did not worship as commanded. Do you know what they were doing? They were watching to see Shadrach, Meshach, and Abednego. If they themselves had bowed their faces to the ground, according to Nebuchadnezzar's command, they would not have seen that Daniel's three friends refused to bow: they would not have seen the three young Hebrews standing up, erect, straight. There were those Chaldeans looking out of the corners of their eyes, and watching the three young men. These young Jews had so carried themselves, and had so lived in Babylon, that their watchers felt sure they would not bow down. They knew well that the three would not sacrifice principle. They would go as far as it was lawful in obeying the king's commands; but a time would come when they would draw the line. When the commands of the earthly sovereign come in conflict with the commands of the God of Heaven they will not yield. The watchers watched; but the young men did not bow. Thank God, they had backbone, if you will allow me the expression. Something held their knees firm; they would not give in: there they stood as firm as rock. They did not get half-way down, and just make believe that they were going to worship the image: there was nothing of that kind: they stood up erect and firm.

Some of those Chaldeans wished to get rid of these young Hebrews: they perhaps wanted their places: they were after their offices. Men have been the same in all ages. There were, no doubt, a good many men in Babylon who wanted to get their posts. These three men had high positions; there was a good deal of honor attached to their offices: and their enemies wanted to oust them, and to succeed to their offices. It is a very bad state of things when men try to pull down others in order to obtain their places; and there is a good deal of that, you know, in this world. Many a man has had his character blasted and ruined by some person or other who wanted to step into his place and position.

So away went those men to the king to lay an information. They duly rendered the salutation, "O king, live forever!" and then they went on to tell him of those rebellious Hebrews who would not obey the king's order. "Do you know, O king, that there are three men in your kingdom who will not obey your command?"

"Three men who will not obey me!" roars Nebuchadnezzar; no! who are they? what are their names?"

"Why, those three Hebrew slaves whom you set over us - Shadrach, Meshach, and Abednego. When the music struck up they did not bow down; and it is noised all around: the people know it. And if you allow them to go unpunished, it will not be long before your law will be perfectly worthless."

I can imagine the king almost speechless with rage, and just gesturing his commands that the men should be brought before him. "Is it true, O Shadrach, Meshach, and Abednego, that you would not bow down and worship the golden image which I set up in the plain of Dura?"

"It is true, quite true, says one of them" - perhaps Shadrach. "Quite true, O king."

One last chance Nebuchadnezzar resolved to give them. "Now, if ye be ready that at what time ye hear the sound of the cornet, flute, harp, sackbut, psaltery, and dulcimer, and all kinds of music, ye fall down and worship the image which I have made - well: but if ye worship not, ye shall be cast the same hour into the midst of a burning fiery furnace. And who is that God that shall deliver you out of my hands?"

That is pretty plain speaking, is it not? There is no mincing or smoothing over matters. Do this, and live; do not do it, and you die. But the threat that the king held out had few terrors for them. They turned and said to the king: "O Nebuchadnezzar, we are not careful to answer thee in this matter. If it be so, our God whom we serve is able to deliver us from the burning fiery furnace; and He will deliver us out of thine hand, O king. But if not, be it known unto thee, O king, that we will not serve thy gods, nor worship the golden image which thou hast set up."

And that is plain speaking, too. The king of Babylon had not been accustomed to be talked to like that. And he did not like it. We are told he was full of fury.

These Hebrews spoke respectfully, but firmly. And mark, they did not absolutely say that God would deliver them from the burning fiery furnace; but they declared that He was able to deliver them. They had no doubt about His ability to do it. They believed that He would do it; but they did not hide from themselves the possibility of Nebuchadnezzar being allowed to carry out his threats. Still, that did not greatly move them. But if not - if in His inscrutable purposes He allows us to suffer - still our resolve is the same: we will not serve thy gods, nor worship the golden image which thou hast set up. They were not afraid to pass from the presence of the king of Babylon to the presence of the King of kings. They had courage, those men. I wonder if there could be found three such brave men in New York, or in Boston, or in Baltimore, or in Chicago, now. How settled they were in their minds! Thank God for such courage! thank God for such boldness! A few such men, brave and fearless for God, would soon turn the world upside down. Nowadays they would be thought fanatics: they would be advised to bow down outwardly, and never to mind the worship of the image. But even the semblance of worshipping an image was too much for them; and they were determined to avoid even the appearance of evil.

Look at the king! I can imagine him in his fury, trembling like an aspen leaf, and turning pale as death with rage. "What! disobey me, the great and mighty king? Call in the mighty men; and let them bind these rebels hand and foot. Heat the furnace seven times hotter than its wont; and then in with these rebellious fellows! They shall not live."

"Then these men were bound in their coats, their hosen, and their hats, and their other garments, and were cast into the midst of the burning fiery furnace."

The command was instantly executed; and they were hurled into the terrible blaze. The fire was so furious that the flames consumed the officers who thrust them in. The three young Hebrews fell down bound into the midst of the burning fiery furnace; and it seemed as if they were in a bad case then. From his royal seat the king peered forth, looking out to see the rebels burnt to ashes. But when Nebuchadnezzar gazed, expecting the gratification of his vengeance, to his great amazement he saw the men walking about in the midst of the flames; walking, mind you - they were not running - walking as if in the midst of green pastures or on the margin of still waters. There was no difference in them, except that their bonds were burnt off. Ah, it does my heart good to think that the worst the devil is allowed to do is to burn off the bonds of God's children. If Christ be with us, the direst afflictions can only loosen our earthly bonds, and set us free to soar the higher.

Nebuchadnezzar beheld strange things that day. There, through the flames, he saw FOUR men walking in the midst of the fire, although only three had been cast therein. How was this? The Great Shepherd in yonder Heaven saw that three of His lambs were in trouble; and He leaped down from there right into the fiery furnace. And when Nebuchadnezzar looked in, a fourth form was to be seen.

"Did not we cast three men bound into the midst of the fire? They answered and said unto the king, True, O king. He answered and said, Lo, I see four men loose, walking in the midst of the fire, and they have no hurt; and the form of the fourth is like the Son of God."

It was doubtless the Son of God. That Great Shepherd of the sheep saw that three of His true servants were in peril; and He came from His Father's presence and His Father's bosom to be with them in it. There had been One watching that terrible scene of attempting to burn the faithful; and His tender pitying eye saw that men were condemned to death because of their loyalty to Him. With one great leap He sprang from the Father's presence, from His palace in glory, right down into the fiery furnace, and was by their side before the heat of the fire could come near unto them. Jesus was with His servants as the flames wreathed around them. And not a hair of their heads was singed; they were not scorched; not even the smell of fire was upon them. I can almost fancy I hear them chanting: "When thou passest through the waters I will be with thee; and through the rivers, they shall not overflow thee; when thou walkest through the fire, thou shalt not be burned; neither shall the flame kindle upon thee."

God can take care of us when we pass through the waters; God can take care of us when we pass through the fires. God is able to take care of us, if we will but stand up for Him: God will take care of us, if we will but stand up for Him. Young man, honor God; and God will honor you. What you have to do is to take your stand upon God's side. And if you have to go against the whole world, take that stand.

Dare to do right; dare to be true; dare to be honest: let the consequences be what they may. You may have to forfeit your situation; because you cannot, and will not, do something which your employer requires you to do, but which your conscience tells you is wrong. Give up your situation then, rather than give up your principles. If your employer requires you to sell goods by means of misrepresentation, fraud, or falsehood, give up your situation, and say, I will rather die a pauper; I will rather die in a poorhouse; than be unfaithful to my principles. That is the kind of stuff those men were made of. These glorious heroes braved even death because God was with them. O friends, we want to be Christians with the same backbone: men and women who are prepared to stand up for the right, heeding not what the world may say or what the world may think.

"Then Nebuchadnezzar came near to the mouth of the burning fiery furnace, and spoke, and said, Shadrach, Meshach, and Abednego, ye servants of the Most High God, come forth, and come hither." And they walked out, untouched by the fire. They came out, like giants in their conscious strength. I can fancy how the princes, the governors, the counselors, and the great men, crowded around them to see such an unheard-of sight. Their garments showed no trace of fire; their hair even was not singed - as if God would teach that He guards even the very hairs of our head. Nebuchadnezzar had defied God; and had been conquered. God had proved Himself able to deliver His servants out of the king's hand. Nebuchadnezzar accepted his defeat. And he makes a decree: "That every people, nation, and language, which speak anything against the God of Shadrach, Meshach, and Abednego, shall be cut in pieces, and their houses shall be made a dunghill: because there is no other God that can deliver after this sort."

And he promoted these three witnesses to higher place and position, and put greater honor upon them. God stood by them because they had stood by Him. He will have us learn to do a thing just because it is right, and not because it is popular. The outlook may appear like death: but do the right; and, if we stand firm, God will bring everything for the best. That is the last we hear of these three men. God sent them to Babylon to shine - and they shone.

LIVING! WORKING! WAITING!

Who would not live for Jesus,
Rejoicing, glad and free?
The music of a ransomed life
Is all He asks from thee.

Who would not work for Jesus,
When service is but song?
The rippling of a stream of love
That bears thy soul along?

Who would not die for Jesus,
When death is victory?
The grand, overshadowing portal-gate
Guarding eternity?

Who would not wait for Jesus,
And waiting, sweetly sing?
Hushing their heart with promises
While tarrying for their King?
- Eva Travers Poole

CHAPTER 4: NEBUCHADNEZZARS SECOND DREAM

"I, Nebuchadnezzar, was at rest in mine house, and flourishing in my palace: I saw a dream which made me afraid, and the thoughts upon my bed and the visions of my head troubled me" (Daniel 4:5)

BY AND BY Nebuchadnezzar had another dream. Surely this man will be brought to see God's hand at last. How many signs and wonders has he seen, fitted to convince him of God's mighty power! This time he remembers the particulars of the dream well enough: they stand out vivid and clear to his mind. Again he calls in the four classes of men on whom he counts to make dark things light, and hidden things plain; and he recounts to them the incidents of this dream. But the magicians, the astrologers, the Chaldeans, and the soothsayers, are all at fault: they cannot tell him the interpretation. When called upon to interpret his former dream they all stood silent. And they stood silent again as the second dream is unfolded to them. There was something in these dreams of the king which stopped their mouths - usually so ready with some plausible interpretation. With these royal dreams it was no use: they were beaten.

It would appear that Nebuchadnezzar had half-forgotten the man who had recounted to him his former dream, and given its interpretation. He says, "At last Daniel came before me. And he proceeds to address Daniel by his Chaldean name of Belteshazzar. O Belteshazzar, master of the magicians, because I know that the spirit of the holy gods is in thee, and no secret troubleth thee, tell me the visions of my dream that I have seen, and the interpretation thereof. Thus were the visions of mine head in my bed; I saw, and behold a tree in the midst of the earth, and the height thereof was great. The tree grew, and was strong; and the height thereof reached unto Heaven, and the sight thereof to the end of all the earth: the leaves thereof were fair and the fruit thereof much, and in it was meat for all: the beasts of the field had shadow under it, and the fowls of the Heaven dwelt in the boughs thereof, and all flesh was fed of it. I saw in the visions of my head upon my bed; and behold, a watcher and an holy one came down from Heaven: he cried aloud, and said thus, Hew down the tree and cut off his branches, shake off his leaves, and scatter his fruit: let the beasts get away from under it, and the fowls from his branches: nevertheless leave the stump of his roots in the earth, even with a band of iron and brass, in the tender grass of the field; and let it be wet with the dew of Heaven, and let his portion be with the beasts in the grass of the earth:

let his heart be changed from mans, and let a beasts heart be given unto him; and let seven times pass over him. This matter is by the decree of the watchers, and the demand by the word of the holy ones: to the intent that the living may know that the Most High ruleth in the kingdom of men, and giveth it to whomsoever He will, and setteth up over it the basest of men. This dream I, King Nebuchadnezzar, have seen. Now thou, O Belteshazzar, declare the interpretation thereof, forasmuch as all the wise men of my kingdom are not able to make known unto me the interpretation: but thou art able: for the spirit of the holy gods is in thee."

As soon as the prophet appears upon the scene the king feels sure that he will now get the meaning of the dream.

For a time Daniel stands still and motionless. Does his heart fail him? The record simply says "he was astonished for one hour; and his thoughts troubled him." He saw what was meant by the royal dream - that the king was to have a terrible fall; and that the kingdom was, at least for a season, to be taken from this proud monarch. The ready words rush to his lips; but he hates to let them out. He does not want to tell Nebuchadnezzar that his kingdom and his mind are both about to depart from him; and that he is to wander forth to eat grass like a beast. The king, too, hesitates: a dark foreboding for a time gets the better of his curiosity. But soon he nerves himself to hear the worst; and in kindly words desires Daniel to proceed, to tell out all he knows. And Daniel breaks the silence. He does not smooth over the matter; but speaks out plainly. There and then he preached righteousness to the king. A very good sermon it was too that he preached. If we had more of the same sort now it would be the better for us. He entreats the king to break off his sins by righteousness, and his iniquities by showing mercy to the poor: if it may be a lengthening of thy tranquility.

Perhaps he told him, for his encouragement, how the King of Nineveh, more than two centuries before, had repented at the preaching of Jonah. He unfolds the full meaning of the dream. He tells the king that the great and strong tree symbolizes Nebuchadnezzar himself; and that just as the tree was hewn down and destroyed, so will he himself be shorn of power and robbed of strength. Daniel tells him that he will be driven from among men, and have to herd with the beasts of the field: yet that nevertheless the kingdom should in the end revert to him, just as the great watcher had spared the stump of the tree.

Repentance might have deferred, or even averted, the threatened calamity. But at that time he repented not. And twelve months afterwards the king heedless of the prophetic warning, and lifted up with pride, walked either through the corridors of his great palace, or out upon its roof; looked forth upon the city's vast extent; gazed at those hanging gardens which counted as one of the wonders of the world; and said: "Is not this great Babylon, that I have built for the house of the kingdom, by the might of my power, and for the honor of my majesty?"

A voice from Heaven instantly cried, "The kingdom is departed from thee." And then and there God touched his reason: it reeled and tottered on its throne, and fled. He was driven forth from men; he herded with animals; his body was wet with the dew of Heaven. This greatest of princes had gone clean mad. It would not take me fifteen minutes today to prove that the world has gone clean mad; and the mass of professing Christians too. Do not men think and talk as everything were done by their own power? Is not God completely forgotten? Do not men neglect every warning that He in mercy sends? Yes, men are mad, and nothing short of it.

NEBUCHADNEZZAR'S REPENTANCE.

But Nebuchadnezzar's kingdom had not passed away from him irrevocably; for, according to the prophets word, at the close of the seven times his understanding returned to him; he resumed his throne and his authority; and his counselors and officers again gathered around him. His power has been given back to him; and he is now a very different man. Of a truth the king's reason has returned to him; and he is possessed of a very different spirit. He sends forth a new proclamation giving honor to the Most High, and extolling the God of Heaven. Its closing words show his repentance, and tend to prove that Daniel had brought this mighty king to God.

It is interesting to go over the different proclamations of Nebuchadnezzar, and note the change that takes place in them. He sent out one proclamation setting forth what other people ought to do, and how they should serve the God of these Hebrews. But the truth did not get home to himself until now. Here is his closing proclamation: "At the end of the days, I, Nebuchadnezzar, lifted up mine eyes unto Heaven, and mine understanding returned unto me; and I blessed the Most High, and I praised and honored Him that liveth forever, whose dominion is an everlasting dominion, and His kingdom is from generation to generation. At the same time my reason returned unto me: and for the glory of my kingdom, mine honor and brightness returned unto me; and my counselors, and my lords sought unto me: and I was established in my kingdom, and excellent majesty was added unto me. Now I, Nebuchadnezzar, praise and extol and honor the King of Heaven, all whose works are truth, and His ways judgment: and those that walk in pride He is able to abase."

When you find that a man has got to praising God it is a good sign. The earlier edict said much about other peoples duty towards the God of the Hebrews, but nothing about what the king himself should do. Oh, let us get to personal love, personal praise! That is what is wanted in the church in the present day. Nebuchadnezzar passes from the stage: this is the last record we have of him. But we may surely hope that, like that of the Corinthians, his was a repentance to salvation not to be repented of. And if this were so we may well believe that today Nebuchadnezzar the king and Daniel the captive are walking the crystal pavement of Heaven arm-in-arm together; and, it may be, talking over the old times in Babylon. Now, if the young prophet had been of a vacillating character; if he had been of a willowy growth, liable to be shaken by every wind, and had not stood there in that city like a great oak - do you think he would have won this mighty monarch to his religion and his God? As a result of that young man going to that heathen city and standing firm for his God, and the God of the Bible, the Lord honored him, and gave him that mighty monarch as a star in his crown. We may fairly say that King Nebuchadnezzar was led to the God of the Hebrews through the faith of this Hebrews love - just because he had

> "a purpose firm,
> And dared to make it known."

THE MASTERS SERVICE.

Service of Jesus! Oh, service of sweetness!
There are no bonds in that service for me;
Full of delight and most perfect completeness:
Evermore His, yet so joyously free!
Service of Jesus! Oh, service of power!
Sharing His glory, while sharing His shame!
All the best blessings the Master can shower
Rest on the servant exalting His name.
Service of Jesus! Oh, service joy-giving!
Melting our hearts into rivers of love;
Secret of life and the sweetness of living,
Joy felt on earth that will fill us above.
Service of Jesus! Oh, service of praising!
Such as redeemed ones rejoicing can sing,
Daily and hourly their voices upraising,
Lauding their Savior, extolling their King.

Eva Travers Poole.

CHAPTER 5: THE HANDWRITING ON THE WALL.

"Belshazzar the king made a great feast to a thousand of his lords, and drank wine before the thousand" (Daniel 5.1)

AND NOW, FOR twenty long years or more, we lose sight of Daniel. He may possibly have been for a portion of the interval living in retirement; but at the end of it he still appears to be holding some appointment at the Babylonish court; although most likely occupying a less prominent position than of yore. Nebuchadnezzar had died; and there was now ruling in Babylon, or it may be acting in some such position as Regent, a young man whose name was Belshazzar. This youthful ruler made a great feast to a thousand of his lords, and drank wine before the thousand. Of this prince we only get a single glimpse. This scene of the feast is the first and last view we have of him; and it is enough. How long that banqueting lasted we do not know; but in the East feasts often extend over many days. Amongst the Jews seven days was not an unusual time for the duration of a feast, and occasionally the time was extended to twice seven days, i.e., fourteen days. It was a great feast. The king caroused with his satraps and princes, his lords, and the mighty men of Babylon, together with his wives and concubines, drinking and rioting, and praising the gods of gold, and of silver, of brass, of iron, of wood, and of stone. That is pretty much what men are doing today, if they are bowing their knee to the God of this world. Cyrus, the great Persian general, is outside the gates, besieging the city, just as Nebuchadnezzar had besieged Jerusalem. And this Belshazzar fancies himself secure behind the lofty and massive walls that encompass Babylon.

The revelers wax daring and wanton. They had forgotten the power of the God of the Hebrews, as shown in the days of Nebuchadnezzar. Heated with wine and lifted up with pride, they laid their sacrilegious hands on the golden vessels which had been brought out of the temple of the house of God which was at Jerusalem; and out of those sacred cups they drank. And as they drank to their idols, one can readily believe that they scoffed at the God of Israel. I could almost picture the scene before me now, and can imagine I hear them blaspheming His holy name. Now they make merry; now they are in the midst of their boisterous revelry. But lo! stop! What is the matter? The king is struck by something that he sees! His countenance has changed. He has turned deadly pale! The wine cup has fallen from his grasp! His knees smite together. He trembles from head to foot. I should not wonder if his lords and nobles did not laugh in their sleeve at him, thinking he was drunk. But, there, along the wall, standing out in living light, are seen letters of strange and unintelligible shape. In the same hour came forth fingers of a mans hand, and wrote over against the candlestick upon the plaster of the wall of the king's palace; and the king saw the part of the hand that wrote.

Above the golden candlestick, on a bare space of the wall, Belshazzar beholds that mysterious handwriting. He distinctly discerns the tracing of those terrible words. Was that writing on the palace wall the work of the same hand that had traced the tables of stone at Sinai? Or did some angel messenger execute the Divine commission? The words, fingers of a mans hand, seem to imply the latter.

The king cries aloud, and commands that the astrologers, the Chaldeans, and the soothsayers, should be brought forward. They come trooping in; and he says to them: Whosoever shall read this writing, and show me the interpretation thereof, shall be clothed with scarlet (or purple), and have a chain of gold about his neck, and shall be the third ruler in the kingdom. One after another tries to spell out that writing; but they fail to understand it. They are skilled in Chaldean learning; but this inscription baffles them. They cannot make out the meaning, any more than an unrenewed man can make out the Bible. They do not understand God's writing: they cannot comprehend it. A man must be born of the Spirit before he can understand God's Book or God's writing. No uncircumcised eyes could decipher those words of fire.

The queen hears of the state of affairs, and comes in to encourage and advise. She salutes the king with the words, O king, live forever! let not thy thoughts trouble thee, nor let thy countenance be changed; and then she goes on to tell him that there is one man in the kingdom who will be able to read the writing, and tell out its meaning. She proceeds to say that in the days of Nebuchadnezzar, light, and understanding, and wisdom, like the wisdom of the gods, was found in him; and advises that Daniel shall be summoned.

For some - perhaps several - years he may have been comparatively little known: may have dropped out of notice, as we say. But now, for the third time, he stands before a Babylonian ruler to interpret and to reveal, when the powers of its magicians and astrologers have utterly failed. Daniel comes in; and his eye lights up as he sees the letters upon the wall. He can read the meaning of the words. The king puts forth his offer of rewards; but Daniel is unmoved: Let thy gifts be to thyself, and give thy rewards to another: yet I will read the writing unto the king, and make known to him the interpretation.

But before he reads the words upon the wall he gives the king a bit of his mind. Perhaps he had been long praying for an opportunity of warning him; and now he has it, he will not let it slip, although all those mighty lords are there. So he reminds the king of the lessons he ought to have learned from the visitation that fell upon the mighty Nebuchadnezzar: of how that monarch had been humbled, brought down, and deposed from his kingly throne, because his heart was lifted up, and his mind hardened in pride; until at length he came to repentance, and realized that the Most High God ruleth in the kingdom of men. "And thou his son, O Belshazzar, hast not humbled thine heart, though thou knewest all this; but hast lifted up thyself against the Lord of Heaven."

Then looking up at the mystic words standing forth in their lambent light, he reads:

"MENE, MENE, TEKEL, UPHARSIN"

MENE: God hath numbered thy kingdom, and finished it.
TEKEL: Thou art weighed in the balances, and art found wanting.
UPHARSIN: Thy kingdom is divided, and given to the Medes and Persians.

How the word of doom must have rung through the palace that night! There was an awful warning. Sinner, it is for you. What if God should put you in the balance, and you without Christ! What would become of your soul? Take warning by Belshazzar's fate.

The destruction did not tarry. The king thought he was perfectly secure: he considered that the walls of Babylon were impregnable. But in that night, at the very hour when Daniel was declaring the doom of the king, Cyrus, the conquering Persian, was turning the Euphrates from its regular course and channel, and was bringing his army within those gigantic walls: the guard around the palace is beaten back; the Persian soldiers force their way to the banqueting-hall; and Belshazzar's blood flows mingling with the outpoured wine upon the palace floor.

It was Belshazzar's last night. One short chapter gives us all we know of that young monarch. His life was short. The wicked do not live out half their days. An impious young man, he had neglected or forgotten the holy Daniel: he had set aside his fathers counselor and friend: he had turned away from the best adviser and most faithful servant that Nebuchadnezzar had ever had - one who probably had done more than anyone else to build up and consolidate his kingdom. And this is his end.

O sinners, take warning: Death and hell are right upon you - death and hell, I say. And they are just as close, it may be, as was the sword of the slayer to those midnight revelers.

CHAPTER 6: THE EDICT OF DARIUS.

"To establish a royal statute, and to make a firm decree, that whosoever shall ask a petition of any God or man for thirty days, save of thee, O king, he shall be cast into the den of lions" (Daniel 6:7)

WE FIND THAT DARIUS - who was probably one of the high military commanders engaged in the siege of Babylon - takes the kingdom, while Cyrus is off conquering other parts of the world. As soon as he attains the throne he makes his arrangements for governing the country. He divides the kingdom into one hundred and twenty provinces; and he appoints a prince or ruler over each province; and over the princes he puts three presidents to see that these rulers do no damage to the king, and do not swindle the government. And over these three he places Daniel, as president of the presidents. Very possibly Darius knew the man. He may have been in former days at the court of Nebuchadnezzar; and if so, he probably considered Daniel an able and conscientious statesman. Anyhow, the king either knew, or was told, sufficient to justify his confidence. And now Daniel is again in office. He held in that day the highest position, under the sovereign, that anyone could hold. He was next to the throne. If you will allow me the expression, he was the Bismarck or the Gladstone of the empire. He was Prime Minister; he was Secretary of State; and all important matters would pass through his hands.

We do not know how long he held that position. But sooner or later the other presidents and the princes grew jealous, and wanted Daniel out of the way. It was as if they had said, "Let us see if we cannot get this sanctimonious Hebrew removed: he has bossed us long enough." You see he was so impracticable: they could do nothing with him. There were plenty of collectors and treasurers; but he kept such a close eye on them that they only made their salaries. There was no chance of plundering the government while he was at the head. He was president, and probably all the revenue accounts passed before him. No doubt these enemies wanted to form a ring. And they may have talked somewhat after this fashion: "If it were not for this man we could form a ring; and then, in three or four years, we could make enough to enable us to retire from office, and have a villa on the banks of the Euphrates; or we could go down to Egypt, and see something of the world. We could have plenty of money - all we should ever want, or our children either - if we could only just get control of the government, and manage things as we should like to. As things go now we only just get our exact dues; and it will take years and years for them to mount up to anything respectable. If we had matters in our own hands it would be different; for King Darius does not know half as much about the affairs of this empire as does this old Hebrew: and he watches our accounts so closely that we can get no advantage over the Government. Down with this pious Jew!"

Perhaps they worked matters so as to get an investigating committee, hoping to catch him in his accounts. But it was no use. If he had put any relatives in office unfairly it would have been found out. And if he had been guilty of peculation, or in any way broken the unalterable laws of the kingdom, the matter would have come to light.

Now I want to call your attention to the fact that one of the highest eulogies ever paid to a man on earth was pronounced upon Daniel at this time by his enemies. These men were connected with the various parts of the kingdom, and on laying their heads together they came to this conclusion - that they could find no occasion against this Daniel, except they found it against him concerning the law of his God. What a testimony from his bitterest enemies! Would that it could be said of all of us! He had never taken a bribe: he had never been connected with a ring: he had never planted a friend into some fat office with the design of sharing the plunder and enriching himself. If he had been guilty in any of these things these scrutineers would have found it out: they had a keen scent: they were sharp men: they knew all about his actions and his history: and they would have been glad to have found out something - anything - which would have led to his removal from his high position. But they said - and said with regret: We shall not find any occasion against him. Ah, how his name shines! He had commenced to shine in his early manhood; and he shone right along. Now he is an old man, an old statesman; and yet this is their testimony. There had been no sacrifice of principle in order to catch votes; no buying up of men's votes or men's consciences; no counting in or counting out. There had been none of that. He had walked right straight along.

Young man, character is worth more than money. Character is worth more than anything else in the wide world. I would rather in my old age have such a character as that which Daniel's enemies gave him than have raised over my dead body a monument of gold reaching from earth to sky. I would rather have such a testimony as that borne of Daniel than have all this world can give.

The men said, We will get him out of the way. We will get the king to sign a decree; and we will propose a penalty. It shall not be the fiery furnace this time. We will have a lions den - a den of angry lions; and they will soon make away with him. Probably these plotters met at night, for it generally happens that if men want to do any downright mean business they meet at night: darkness suits them best. The chief-president himself was not there: he had not been invited to meet them. Very likely some lawyer, who understood all about the laws of the Medes and Persians, stood up, and talked something after this fashion: Gentlemen, I have got, I think, a plan that will work well, by which we may get rid of this old Hebrew. You know he will not serve any but the God of Abraham and of Isaac.

We know that very well. And if a man had gone to Babylon in those days he would not have had to ask if Daniel loved the God of the Bible. I pity any man who lives so that people have to ask, Is he a Christian? Let us so live that no one need ask that question about us. These men knew very well that Daniel worshipped none other than the God of the Bible, the God of the Hebrews, the God of Abraham, and the God of Moses; the God who had brought His people Israel out of Egypt, through the Red Sea, and into the Promised Land: they knew that very well.

And these plotters said one to another, Now, let us get Darius to sign a decree that if any man make a request of any God or man - except of the King Darius - for thirty days, he shall be put into the lions den. And let us all keep perfectly still about this matter, so that it won't get out. We must not tell our wives, for fear the news may get about the city: Daniel would find it all out; and he has more influence with the king than all the rest of us put together. The king would never sign the decree if he found out what the object was. Then they may have said, We must draw it so tight that Darius will not be able to get out of it after he has once signed. We must make it so binding that if the king once signs we shall have that Daniel in the lions den: and we will take good care that the lions shall be hungry.

When the mine is all ready, the conspirators come to the king, and open their business with flattering speech: King Darius, live forever! When people approach me with smooth and oily words, I know they have something else coming - I know they have some purpose in telling me I am a good man. These plotters, perhaps, go on to tell the king how prosperous the realm is, and how much the people think of him. And then, perhaps, in the most plausible way, they tell him that if he signs this decree he will be remembered by their children's children - that it would be a memorial forever of his greatness and goodness. "What is this decree that you wish me to sign?" And running his eye over the document he says, "I don't see any objection to that." "Will you put your signet to it, and make it law?" He puts his signature to the decree, and seals it with his seal. And one of them says, "The law of the Medes and Persians, which altereth not?" and the king answers, "Oh, yes; the law of the Medes and Persians: that is it." In the pleasure of granting the request of these people he thinks nothing about Daniel; and the presidents and princes carefully refrain from jogging his memory. They had told the king a lie, too; for they said, ALL the presidents of the kingdom, the governors, and the princes, the counselors, and the captains, have consulted together to establish a royal statute; although the chief-president knew nothing at all about it.

There was probably a long preamble, telling him how popular he was; saying that he was liked better than Nebuchadnezzar or Belshazzar. They most likely tickled his vanity, and told him that he was the most popular man that had ever reigned in Babylon; and then they may have gone on to tell him how attached they were to him and his rule, and that they had been consulting together what they could do to increase his popularity and make him more beloved; and now they had hit upon a plan that was almost sure to do it. They would point out that if no one called upon any God for thirty days, but only on him, the king, making him a God, it would render him the most popular monarch that had ever reigned in Babylonia; and his name would be handed down to posterity. And if he could get men to call upon his name for thirty days they would probably keep it up, and so permanently reckon him among the gods.

If you touch a mans vanity he will do almost anything; and Darius was like most of the human race. They touched his vanity by intimating that this would make him great. He thought it a very wise suggestion, and he agreed with them exactly.

It was not only Daniel they were thus going to get out of the way, but every conscientious Jew. There was not a true Jew in the whole of that wide empire who would bow down and worship Darius; and these men knew that: and so they were going to sweep away at a stroke all the Jews who were true to their faith. They hated them. And I want to tell you that the world does not love Christians nowadays. The world will persecute a man if he attempts to live the life of a true Christian. The world is no friend to true grace: mark that! A man may live for the world, and like the world, and escape persecution. But if the world has nothing to say against you, it is a pretty sure sign that God has not much to say for you; because if you do seek to live unto Christ Jesus you must go against the current of the world. And now they are ready to let the news go forth; and it is not long before it spreads through the highways of Babylon. The men of the city knew the man: knew that he would not vacillate. They knew that the old man with the gray locks would not turn to the right hand or the left: they knew that if his enemies caught him in that way, he would not deny his God or turn away from Him: they knew that he was going to be true to his God.

Daniel was none of your sickly Christians of the nineteenth century: he was none of your weak-backed, none of your weak-kneed Christians: he had moral stamina and courage. I can imagine that aged white-haired Secretary of State sitting at his table going over the accounts of some of these rulers of provinces. Some of the timid, frightened Hebrews come to him, and say:

"Oh, Daniel, have you heard the latest news?"

"No. What is it?"

"What! have you not been to the king's palace this morning? No! I have not been to the palace today. What is the matter?"

"Well, there is a conspiracy against you. A lot of those princes have induced King Darius to sign a decree that if any man shall call upon any God in his kingdom within thirty days he shall be thrown to the lions. Their object is to have you cast into the den. Now if you can only get out of the way for a little time - if you will just quit Babylon for thirty days - it will advance both your own and the public interest. You are the chief secretary and treasurer - in fact, you are the principal member of the government: you are an important man, and can do as you please. Well now, just you get out of Babylon. Or, if you will stay in Babylon, do not let any one catch you on your knees. In any case do not pray at the window which looks towards Jerusalem; as you have been doing for the last fifty years. And if you will pray, close that window, draw a curtain over it; shut the door, and stop up every crevice. People are sure to be about your house listening."

And some of our nineteenth century Christians would have advised after the same fashion: "Cannot you find out some important business to be done down in Egypt, and so take a journey to Memphis? or can you not think of something that needs being looked after in Syria, and so hurry off to Damascus? Or, surely you can make out there is a need for your going to Assyria, and you can make a stay at Nineveh. Or why not get as far as Jerusalem, and see what changes fifty or sixty years have wrought? Anyway, just be out of Babylon for the next thirty days, so that your enemies may not catch you: for, depend upon it, they will all be on the watch. And, whatever you do, be sure they do not catch you on your knees."

How many men there are who are ashamed to be caught upon their knees! Many a man, if found upon his knees by the wife of his bosom, would jump right up and walk around the room as if he had no particular object in view. How many young men there are who come up from the country and enter upon city life, and have not the moral courage to go down on their knees before their roommates! How many young men say, "Don't ask me to get down on my knees at this prayer meeting." Men have not the moral courage to be seen praying. They lack moral courage. Ah! thousands of men have been lost for lack of moral courage; have been lost because at some critical moment they shrank from going on their knees, and being seen and known as being worshippers of God - as being on the Lord's side. Ah, the fact is - we are a pack of cowards: that is what we are. Shame on the Christianity of the nineteenth century! it is a weak and sickly thing. Would to God that we had a host of men like Daniel living today!

I can picture that aged man, with his gray hairs upon him, listening to the words of these miserable counselors, who would tempt him to trim, and hedge, and shift - to save his skin, as men say, at the cost of his conscience. And their counsel falls flat and dead. I can fancy how Daniel would receive a suggestion that he should even seemingly be ashamed of the God of his fathers. Will he be ashamed or afraid? Not likely! You know he will not; and I know he will not.

"They will be watching you; they will have their spies all around. But if you are determined to go on praying, shut up your window; close all your curtains; stop up the keyhole, so that no one can look through to see you on your knees, and so that no one can overhear a single word. Accommodate yourself just a little. Compromise just a little."

That is just the cry of the world today! It is, Accommodate yourself to the times. Compromise just a little here; and deviate just a little there, just to suit the opinions and views of a mocking world. Do you think that Daniel, after having walked with God for half a century or more, is going to turn round like that? Ten thousand times, No!

True as steel, that old man goes to his room three times a day. Mark you, he had time to pray. There is many a business man today who will tell you he has no time to pray: his business is so pressing that he cannot call his family around him, and ask God to bless them. He is so busy that he cannot ask God to keep him and them from the temptations of the present life - the temptations of every day. Business is so pressing I am reminded of the words of an old Methodist minister: If you have so much business to attend to that you have no time to pray, depend upon it you have more business on hand than God ever intended you should have. But look at this man. He had the world, or nearly the whole, of the king's business to attend to. He was Prime Minister, Secretary of State, and Secretary of the Treasury, all in one. He had to attend to all his own work; and to give an eye to the work of lots of other men. And yet he found time to pray: not just now and then, nor once in a way, not just when he happened to have a few moments to spare, mark you - but three times a day. Yes, he could take up the words of the fifty-fifth Psalm, and say:

> As for me, I will call upon God;
> And the Lord shall save me.
> Evening, and morning, and at noon,
> will I pray and cry aloud;
> And He shall hear my voice.

Busy as he was, he found time to pray. And a man whose habit it is to call upon God saves time, instead of losing it. He has a clearer head, a more collected mind, and can act with more decision when circumstances require it.

So Daniel went to his room three times a day: he trod that path so often that the grass could not grow upon it. I would be bound to say those plotters knew whereabouts he would be going to pray: they knew the place where Daniel's prayer was wont to be made; and they were sure they should find him there at his usual hours. And now again he has

> "a purpose firm,
> And dares to make it known."

He goes to pray as aforetime; and he has his windows open. Like Paul, in later days, he knew whom he had believed; like Moses, he saw Him who is invisible. He knew whom he worshipped. There was no need to trace back the church records for years to find out whether this man had ever made a profession of religion. See him as he falls upon his knees. He is not careful to inquire whether there are any outsiders, or whether they can hear. In tones not one atom softer or quieter than his custom, he pours out his prayer to the God of his life; to the God of his people; to the God of Abraham, Isaac, and Jacob. He does not omit to pray for the king. It is right to pray for our rulers. If we cease praying for our rulers, our country will go to pieces. The reason they are not better is oftentimes because we do not pray for them. Does Daniel pray to Darius? Not he! He prays for Darius, but not to him.

There are men listening there near the open window: the hundred and twenty princes have taken good care of that. They themselves are their own witnesses, and some of them gather together as listeners, so doing their own vile work. If there had been any newspaper reporters in that day, how anxious they would have been to have got hold of every word of that prayer! Give them the smallest chance; and they would have taken it down, and telegraphed it all over the world, inside of twenty-four hours.

After Daniel has prayed, and given thanks, - given thanks, mark that! - he goes out, and walks along the street with a firm step. He is undaunted. If it be the will of God that he shall pass from earth to Heaven by the way of the den of lions, he is prepared for that. God's presence is with him. Like Enoch, he bore within himself this testimony – "that he pleased God."

<blockquote>
Do you see the Hebrew captive kneeling,
At morning, noon, and night, to pray?
In his chamber he remembers Zion,
Though in exile far away.
Do not fear to tread the fiery furnace,
Nor shrink the lions den to share;
For the God of Daniel will deliver,
He will send His angel there.
Children of the living God, take courage,
Your great deliverance sweetly sing
Set your faces toward the hill of Zion,
Thence to hail your coming King!
Are your windows open toward Jerusalem,
Though as captives here a little while we stay
For the coming of the King in His glory,
Are you watching day by day.
</blockquote>

CHAPTER 7: THE DEN OF LIONS.

"Then the king commanded, and they brought Daniel, and cast him into the den of lions" (Daniel 6:16)

THERE MUST HAVE BEEN great excitement in the city then: all Babylon knew that this man was not going to swerve. They knew very well that this old statesman was a man of iron will; and that it was not at all likely he would yield. The lions den had few terrors to him. He would rather be in the lions den with God, than out of it without Him. And it is a thousand times better, friends, to be in the lions den with God, and hold to principle - than to be out of it, and have money, but no principle. I pity those men who have gained their money dishonestly; I pity those men who have obtained their positions in life dishonestly; I pity any politician who has acquired his office dishonestly - how his conscience will lash him at times! And how the Word of God lashes such! "Your gold and silver is cankered; and the rust of them shall be a witness against you, and shall eat your flesh as it were fire." It does not pay to be false; it pays to be true. It is best to be honest; even if it means having very little money in our pocket, and very little position in the world. It is best to have God with us, and to know that we are on the right side.

I venture to say that man Daniel was worth more than any other man Darius had in his empire - yes, worth more than forty thousand men who wanted to get him out of the way. He was true to the king. He prayed for him; he loved him; and he did for that king everything he could that did not conflict with the law of his God.

And now the spies rush off to the king, and cry, "O Darius, live forever! Do you know there is a man in your kingdom who will not obey you?"

"A man who won't obey me! Who is he?"

"Why, that man Daniel. That Hebrew whom you set over us. He persists in calling upon his God."

And the moment they mention the name of Daniel, a frown arises upon the king's brow; and the thought flashes into his mind: "Ah! I have made a mistake: I ought never to have signed that decree. I might have known that Daniel would never call upon me. I know very well whom he serves: he serves the God of his fathers." So, instead of blaming Daniel he blames himself: instead of condemning Daniel he condemns himself. And then he casts about in his mind as to how he could manage to preserve him unharmed. All that day, if you could have looked into the palace, you would have seen the king walking up and down the halls and corridors, greatly troubled with the thought that this man must lose his life before the sun sets on that Chaldean plain; for if Daniel were not in the lions den by sundown the law of the Medes and Persians would be broken: and, come what will, that law must be observed and kept. Darius loved Daniel; and he sought in his heart to deliver him. All day he sought for some plan by which he might save Daniel, and yet preserve the Median law unbroken. But he did not love Daniel as much as your King loved you: he did not love him as much as Christ loved us: for if he had he would have proposed to have gone into the lions den in his stead. Let us remember that Christ tasted death for us. I can imagine those plotters having a suspicion as to the king's feelings; and saying to him, If you break the law which you yourself have made, respect for the laws of the Medes and Persians will be gone: your subjects will no longer obey you; and your kingdom will depart from you. So Darius is at last compelled to give him up; and he speaks the word for the officers to seize him and take him to the den. And his enemies would take good care that the den is filled with the hungriest beasts in Babylon.

You might have seen those officers going out to bind that old man with the white flowing hair: they march to his dwelling; and they bind his hands together. And those Chaldean soldiers lead captive the man who a few hours before ranked next to the king; the noblest statesman Babylon had ever possessed. They guard him along the way that leads to the lions den. Look at him as he is led along the streets. He treads with a firm and steady step, bearing himself like a conqueror. He trembles not. His knees are firm: they do not smite together. The light of Heaven shines in his calm face. And all Heaven is interested in that aged man. Disgraced down here upon earth, he is the most popular man in Heaven. Angels are delighted in him: how they love him up there! He had stood firm; he had not deviated; he had not turned away from the God of the Bible. And he walks with a giants tread to the entrance of the lions den; and they cast him in. They roll a great stone to the mouth of the den; and the king puts his seal upon it. And so the law is kept. Daniel is cast into the den; but the angel of God flies down, and God's servant lights unharmed at the bottom. The lions mouths are stopped: they are as harmless as lambs. And if you could have looked into that den, you would have found a man as calm as a summer evening. I do not doubt that at his wonted hour of prayer he knelt down as if he had been in his own chamber. And if he could get the points of the compass in that den, he prayed with his face toward Jerusalem. He loved that city; he loved the temple: and probably with his face toward the city of Jerusalem, he prayed and gave thanks. And later on I can imagine him just laying his head on one of the lions, and going to sleep: and if that were so, no one in Babylon slept more sweetly than Daniel in the den of lions.

But there was one man in Babylon who had no rest that night. If you could have looked into the king's palace, you would have seen one man in great trouble. Darius did not have in his musicians to play to him that night. Away with music and singing! There was no feast that night: he could eat nothing.

The servants brought him dainty food; but he had no appetite for it. He felt troubled: he could not sleep. He had put in that den of lions the best man in his kingdom; and he upbraided himself for it. He said to himself, How could I have been a party to such an act as that?

And early in the morning - probably in the gray dawn, before the sun has risen - the men of Babylon could have heard the wheels of the king's chariot rolling over the pavement; and King Darius might have been seen driving in hot haste to the lions den. I see him alight from his chariot in eager haste, and hear him cry down through the mouth of the den: "O Daniel, servant of the living God, is thy God, whom thou servest continually, able to deliver thee from the lions?"

Hark! a voice gives answer - why, it is like a resurrection voice - and from the depths come up to the king's ear the words of Daniel: "O king, live forever! My God hath sent His angel, and hath shut the lions mouths, that they have not hurt me: forasmuch as before Him innocence was found in me; and also before thee, O king, have I done no hurt."

The lions could not harm him. The very hairs of his head were numbered. I tell you, that whenever a man stands by God, God will stand by him. It was well for Daniel that he did not swerve. Oh, how his name shines! What a blessed character he was! The king gives command that Daniel should be taken up out of the den. And, as he reaches the top, I fancy I see them embracing one another; and that then Daniel mounts the king's chariot, and is driven back with him to the royal palace. There were two happy men in Babylon that morning. Most likely they sat down at meat together, thankful and rejoicing. No manner of hurt was found upon him. The God who had preserved Shadrach, Meshach, and Abednego, in the fiery furnace, so that no smell of fire had passed on them, had preserved Daniel from the jaws of the lions. But Daniel's accusers fared very differently. So to speak, they dug a pit for him; and are fallen into it themselves. The king orders that Daniel's accusers shall be delivered to the same ordeal. And they were cast into the den; and the lions had the mastery of them, and brake all their bones in pieces or ever they came at the bottom of the den.

Young men, let us come out from the world; let us trample it under our feet; let us be true to God; let us stand in rank, and keep step, and fight boldly for our King! And our crowning time shall come by and by. Yes, the reward will come by and by; and then it may perhaps be said of one, or another, of us: O man, greatly beloved! Young men, your moral character is more than money, mark that! It is worth more than the honor of the world: that is fleeting, and will soon be gone. It is worth more than earthly position: that is transient, and will soon be gone. But to have God with you, and to be with God - what a grand position! It is an eternal inheritance.

I should like to say a few more words about Daniel. If you will refer to the tenth chapter, you will read that an angel came to him, and told him he was a man greatly beloved. Another angel had on a previous occasion brought him a similar message. Many are of opinion that the one described in the tenth chapter as appearing to Daniel is none other than the one like unto the Son of Man, who visited John when he was banished to the Isle of Patmos. People thought that John was sent off to that island by himself; but no! the angel of God was with him. And so it was with Daniel, taken from his own country and his own people. Here in this chapter we read: Then I lifted up mine eyes, and looked; and behold a certain man clothed in linen, whose loins were girded with fine gold of Uphaz And he said unto me, O Daniel, a man greatly beloved, understand the words that I speak unto thee; and stand upright: for unto thee am I now sent. It was Daniel's need that brought this angel from the glory-land. And it was the Son of God right by his side in that city of Babylon. As I said before, that was the second time the word had come to him that he was greatly beloved. Aye, and even three times did a messenger come from the throne of God to tell him this.

I love that precious verse in the eleventh chapter: "The people that do know their God shall be strong, and do exploits." And also those two verses of the twelfth chapter: "Many of them that sleep in the dust of the earth shall awake: some to everlasting life; and some to shame and everlasting contempt. And they that be wise shall shine as the brightness of the firmament; and they that turn many to righteousness, as the stars forever and ever." This was the consolation the angel bore to Daniel; and great consolation it was. The fact concerning all of us is that we like to shine. There is no doubt about that. Every mother likes her child to shine. If her boy shines at school by getting to the head of his class, the proud mother tells all the neighbors; and she has a right to do so.

But it is not the great of this world who will shine the brightest. For a few years they may shed bright light: but they go out in darkness; they have no inner light. Shining for a time, they go out in the blackness of darkness. Where are the great men who did not know Daniel's God? Did they shine long? Why, we know of Nebuchadnezzar and the rest of them scarcely anything, except as they fill in the story about these humble men of God. We are not told that statesmen shall shine: they may for a few days or years; but they are soon forgotten. Look at those great ones who passed away in the days of Daniel. How wise in council they were! how mighty and victorious over many nations! what gods upon earth they were! Yet their names are forgotten, and written in the sand. Philosophers, falsely so-called, do they live? Behold men of science - scientific men, they call themselves - going down into the bowels of the earth, hammering away at some rock, and trying to make it talk against the voice of God. They shall go down to death by and by; and their names shall rot. But the man of God shines. Yes, it is he who shall shine as the stars forever and ever.

This Daniel has been gone for 2,500 years; but still increasing millions read of his life and actions. And so it shall be to the end. He will only get better known and better loved; he will only shine the brighter as the world grows older. Of a truth, they that be wise and turn many to righteousness shall shine on, like stars, to eternity.

And this blessed, thrice blessed, happiness, of shining in the glory, is like all the blessings of God's kingdom, for every one. Even without the least claim to education or refinement you can shine if you will. A poor working man, or a poor sailor before the mast, can shine forever, if he only works for the Kingdom of God. The Bible does not say the great shall shine, but they that turn many to righteousness. A false impression has got hold of many of God's people. They have formed the idea that only a few can speak on behalf of God. If anything is to be done for the souls of men, nine-tenths of the people say, Oh, the ministers must do it. It does not enter into the thoughts of many people that they have any part in the matter. It is the devils work to keep Christians from the blessed privilege of winning souls to God. ANY ONE CAN DO THIS WORK.

Do you not see how that little mountain rill keeps swelling till it carries everything before it? Little trickling streams have run into it till now, a mighty river, it has great cities on its banks, and the commerce of all nations floating on its waters. So when a single soul is won to Christ you cannot see the result. A single one multiplies to a thousand; and the thousand into ten thousand. Perhaps a million shall be the fruit. We cannot tell. We only know that the Christian who has turned many to righteousness shall indeed shine forever and ever. Look at those poor, unlettered fishermen, the disciples of Jesus. They were not learned men, but they were great in winning souls. And there is not a child but can work for God.

The one thing that keeps people from working for God is that they have not the desire to do so. If a man has this desire God soon qualifies him. And what we want is God's qualification: it must come from Him.

In our large meetings there are frequently three thousand Christians present. Would it be too much to expect if these were living in communion with Christ that they should each lead one soul to the Lord within a month? The Son of God gave His life for them - shall they refuse to work for Him when He supplies the needed power? What results should we see in souls saved if everyone did his or her work. How many times have I watched at the close of a meeting to see if Christians would speak to the sorrowing ones. If we only had open-eyed watchers for souls, there would be multitudes of inquirers where now there are individual cases. Every church would need an inquiry meeting after every gospel service, and these inquiry rooms would be crowded. These inquiring ones are at every meeting, just anxious to have warm-hearted Christians lead them to Christ. They are timid, but will always listen to one speaking to them about Christ. Let the prayer of every Christian be, Oh God, give me souls for my hire. What would be the result if this were the case with us? Multitudes would be sending up shouts of praise to God, and making Heaven glad. Where there is an anxious sinner, there is the place for the Christian.

WHAT ART THOU DOING?

What art thou doing, Christian?
Is it work for Christ thy Lord?
Art thou winning many sinners
By thy life, thy pen, thy word?
When the solemn question cometh,
What will thine answer be?
Cant thou point to something finished?
Saying - Lord, my work for Thee!

What doest thou in service?
Art thou taking active part
Are life and tongue in earnest,
Outflow of loving heart?
Or art thou idly gazing
While others toil and sow
Content with simply praising
The earnestness they show?

What doest thou, redeemed one,
Child of a mighty King?
What glory to thy Father
Doth thy princely bearing bring?
If no one brought Him honor,
And no one gave Him praise,
To thee it appertaineth
The paean-note to raise.

What doest thou here?
Wherever Thine earthly lot be cast
Oh, let each hour and moment
In gladsome work be passed!
Here! thou mayest do a lifework;
Here! thou mayest win a crown,
Starlit and gem-surrounded,
To cast before the throne.

- Eva Travers Poole.

CHAPTER 8: ENOCH

THE LAST PROPHET of the Jewish dispensation, and almost the last prophet that the world ever had - though Christ, of course, came after him - was John the Baptist. But I now want to call attention to the first prophet who is mentioned in Scripture. You will find an account of him in the fifth of Genesis; "And Jared lived a hundred sixty and two years, and he begat Enoch; and Jared lived after he begat Enoch eight hundred years, and begat sons and daughters. And all the days of Jared were nine hundred sixty and two years: and he died. And Enoch lived sixty and five years, and begat Methuselah. And Enoch walked with God after he begat Methuselah three hundred years, and begat sons and daughters. And all the days of Enoch were three hundred sixty and five years. And Enoch walked with God: and he was not; for God took him."

We find it stated in the book of Jude that Enoch prophesied of the coming of the Lord with ten thousands of his saints; so that we know he was a prophet of the Lord. We find also, in Genesis, another man bearing this name. He was a descendant of Cain, one who built a city, and was, no doubt, very popular and highly thought of by men; whereas, the Enoch we refer to was very unpopular. He who built a city and was so famous, has gone with the city which he built, no one knows where; but the influence of this man, who was gifted with the spirit of prophecy, and who walked with God, is still fresh upon the world.

Enoch lived in a world moulded and fashioned by the sons of Cain. They were the men of light and leading - the men of culture and progress. Jabal took the lead in agriculture; Tubal-Cain was the manufacturer; and Jubal provided the music and amusement. No doubt they thought Enoch an odd man, not valuing the improvements they were making in the sin-blighted earth. They doubtless hated him, because they saw that he despised the paint and varnish with which they were hiding the rottenness of a world dead to God. But they could afford to treat with contempt a minority of one; for they did not perceive the invisible God with whom Enoch walked. But God regarded him; and that satisfied Enoch's soul. He was the one man upon the earth who was well-pleasing in His sight.

Enoch's name - dedicated, disciplined, well-regulated - was significant of his character. He was a dedicated man, whose life was disciplined and his habits regulated by the guiding hand of God. He saw the promises afar off, and was persuaded of them, and embraced them; and by faith lived as one alive from the dead, yielding his members as instruments of righteousness unto God. He strove not about words to no profit, but to the subverting of the hearers; he shunned and purged himself from profane and vain babblings; he was a vessel unto honor, sanctified and meet for the Masters use, and prepared for every good work. Enoch was one of the small number of men against whom nothing is recorded in the Bible. It has been truly said that people think Enoch had not half the trials, half the difficulties, that saints of God have in these days. But that is a very superficial view. Enoch was surrounded by, and going through the midst of, a system of things that Satan has improved upon at the present moment. He lived in the midst of the world as Cain and his descendants had made it. No one supposes that the ordered system of things round about us is the production of God's hand. Satan is the God and prince and head of that... There was a religion and a city. Those were the two great constituent arts of that system of things in which Enoch lived.

Cain was the founder of a religion that disowned the claims of God in righteousness, seeing that man had fallen from God. Cain toiled on the earth, and, though cursed, it yielded its fruit to him; and he brought the fruit of the earth that was cursed, as if there had been no curse at all, and offered it to God. That which characterized and marked the religion of which Cain was the inventor and founder, was bringing to God an offering in such a way as to deny the great principle, that without shedding of blood there is no remission. Then the city is exactly what we have all round us now. There was manufacture; there was the art of man cultivated to its greatest possible extent; ingenuity taxed beyond all conception - to produce something which would make the world, out of which God had been rejected, bearable to man. This was Cain's world. Herein lay its religious, political, and moral aspects.

In the midst of such a state of things, Enoch walked with God; and in the very same world we are also called to walk with God. The record of his life is that he had this testimony, that he pleased God. Notice that this man, the brightest star of all that period of history before the flood, a period which lasted rather more than fifteen hundred years, accomplished nothing that men would call great. He was neither a warrior, a statesman, nor a scientist; nor did he, so far as we know, accomplish anything remarkable, like Daniel, or Joseph, or any of the other mighty men of Israel: but what made him great was that he walked with God. That, in all ages, is what has made men really great. He found the way of holiness in that dark and evil day; and he will be in the front rank of those who shall walk with the Lord, the Lamb, in white, for they are worthy. The faith of Enoch drew God down from Heaven to walk with him. He maintained unbroken fellowship with God. A man in communion with God is one of Heavens greatest warriors. He can battle with and overcome the world, the flesh, and the devil. In this way Enoch was a mighty conqueror. It was not that Enoch was anything; but his God made him great.

Abraham is called the father of all them that believe. Enoch may be called the father of all those who in all generations have walked with God. What made Abraham great? We do not read of any famous speeches that he made, nor that he was a very learned man in the wisdom of the world; but he had faith in Enoch's God, and God walked with him. All down the ages Abraham has been known as the friend of God. Eastern travelers to this day are reminded by the Mohammedans, when approaching Abrahams grave, that he was the friend of God. What made Abraham so great and mighty was that he subdued kingdoms and overcame the world by faith. He was a man of like passions with ourselves; but faith in God made him great.

Joseph was another of those great men who walked in fellowship with God. His brethren tried to get rid of him; Satan attempted to put him down; but they could not although he lay so long in the Egyptian prison. The skeptical and unbelieving of that day might have said, Look at that man; he serves the God of his fathers, the God of Abraham, and Isaac, and Jacob; he will not turn aside a hairs-breadth from the worship of the unknown God: yet see how his God serves him! He is in prison! But wait God's time. It is better to be in prison with God than in a palace without Him. It is said that he was in prison; but - and I like that expression - God was with him. If a man is in communion with God, He will not leave him. God never deserts His children in their hour of need; and, in due time, Joseph came off victorious; exchanged the prison for a throne; and was made ruler over all Egypt. What a power he was in Egypt when God had taken him from prison and put him in his proper place!

Look at Moses. He, too, was in communion with God. When Moses and Aaron stood before Pharaoh, the stubborn king did not see the third Person who was with them. If he had, he might have acted altogether differently. The idea of those two unarmed men going before the mighty monarch of Egypt, and demanding, without trembling for their lives, that he should give three millions of slaves their liberty! The idea of these two men, without position or influence at Court, making such an extraordinary demand as that! But they were in communion with the God of Heaven, and such men always succeed. You must let Israel go, said Moses. Pharaoh mocked. You say your God! What do I care for your God! Who is He that I should obey Him? The king found out who He was. Moses was the mightiest man who lived in his day. Why? Because God walked with him, and he was in communion with God; he was linked to the God of Heaven. Moses alone was nothing. He was a man like you and me; but he was the meekest of men, and the meek shall inherit the earth. He was famous because he walked with his God.

When Elijah stood on Mount Carmel, Ahab did not see who was with him. Little did he know the prophets God; little did he think that, when Elijah walked up Mount Carmel, God walked with him. Talk of an Alexander making the world tremble at the tread of his armies! - of the marches and victories of a Caesar, or a Napoleon! the man who is walking with God is greater than all the Caesars, and Napoleons, and Alexanders, who ever lived. Little did Ahab and the false prophets of Baal know that Elijah was walking with the same God with whom Enoch walked before the Flood. Elijah was nothing when out of communion with God; but when walking in the power of God, he stood on Mount Carmel like a king.

The sword of Gideon was nothing; but away went the Midianites when the Lord linked His power with that of Gideon. When God unites His power with the weakness of His children, they become mighty. It was so when Samson slew a thousand Philistines with the jaw-bone of an ass. We want that same power. Who can stand before a man that, like Enoch, is in communion with God? No one on earth. He is a mighty giant. Strong in the strength which God supplies, he is more than conqueror.

Daniel and his friends had the same God to walk with them in Babylon. The Chaldeans were a mighty people; the king and his warriors had great strength, and had conquered many nations, but Nebuchadnezzar, and Belshazzar, and Darius, and Cyrus, had not the power of Daniel. Why? Because Daniel walked with the God who made Heaven and earth. He was in communion with Him. And when his friends were cast into the fiery furnace, they had nothing to fear. Do you think that God would desert them in that trying hour? I can imagine Shadrach saying to his two companions Be of good cheer. They were probably well acquainted with this prophecy of Isaiah: "When thou passest through the waters, I will be with thee; and through the rivers, they shall not overflow thee. When thou walkest through the fire, thou shalt not be burned; neither shall the flame kindle upon thee." Man is immortal till his work is done. These men had not done their work yet; and the fire could not scorch a hair of their heads, or do them any hurt. The three Hebrew youths were cast into the fire; but the form of a Fourth was with them: God walked with them. Satan had incited the king to make the furnace seven times hotter than usual; but, to Shadrach, Meshach, and Abednego, it was like walking in green pastures, and beside still waters. No hurt can come to those who are walking with God.

Look how it was with Joshua. God told him that no man should be able to stand before him all the days of his life. When the news came to him that a confederacy had been formed against him by five kings, who were bringing against him regiments of giants, and among them the sons of Anak, Joshua was walking with the God of Enoch; he had the same God, and therefore had nothing to fear. When he was told of the danger of encountering them, he was not alarmed; and trusting in the arm of the Lord, he routed all the hosts which were brought against him.

Mark the contrast when there is no communion. Israel rejected God a few hundred years after. They, like other nations, wanted a king who could be seen, and who would go with them to war - instead of the Theocracy with which they were growing discontented. They wanted to walk by sight, not by faith; and when Samuel grieved and wept over them, and remonstrated with them, they said, We will have a king. God directed Samuel to tell them of the consequences, and that they would regret their choice. They had a king who was a head and shoulders above any other man; and they raised the cry, God save the king! When the day of trial came, and when all the armed hosts of Israel were in battle array, out came one solitary giant; and when he shook his finger at them, they all trembled from head to foot. There was not a man in all the army who dare go out and meet him. One giant frightened the whole army. But one at last comes forth who is armed and equipped - for God is with him, which is best of all; and he takes a few small stones and a sling, and goes forth to meet this giant. Was not God with David when he picked up the stones? - when he placed one in the sling, and when he took such a sure aim at the giant of Gath? Yes, he walked with God. We are strong when the Lord is on our side, but weak when we are out of communion.

A great deal is being said about Holiness. Every true child of God desires to be holy, as His Father in Heaven is holy. And holiness is walking with God. Enoch had only one object. How simple life becomes when we have only one object to seek, one purpose to fulfill - to walk with God - to please God! It has been said that the utmost many Christians get to is that they are pardoned criminals. How short they fall of the joy and blessedness of walking with God!

I will venture to say that Enoch, in his day, was considered a most singular and visionary man - an eccentric man - the most peculiar man who lived in that day. He was a man out of fashion - out of the fashion of this world, which passeth away. He was one of those who set their affections on things above. He lived days of Heaven upon earth; for the essence of Heaven is to walk with God. He did not go with the current and the crowd. If the question of drink had been raised, he would have been a teetotaler. He would not have gone with the multitude to do evil. He would have taken that ground, though the whole world were against him. And what we want is the moral courage to be against the whole world when we are in the right. Enoch dared to do right. He took his position, and dared to stand against an ungodly generation. There he stood; and he was not ashamed to stand alone. He testified against the sins of a generation which was filling the earth with violence, and crying out for the judgment of God upon it. While his fellow-men were hurrying toward death and judgment, he calmly walked with God. He took upon him the yoke of the meek and lowly One, and found rest unto his soul.

Enoch was translated fifty-seven years after the death of Adam. He might have been often found in Adams tent; and the young prophet may have talked with him of the second Adam, who would not fall, but would overcome the tempter, and would come with myriads of His holy ones. Perhaps he stood with the ancients round the grave of the father of our race. What a scene must that burial have been! Enoch may have seen the first man who died a natural death, though not the first corpse, nor the first grave, for Abel had been murdered centuries before. But suddenly those antediluvians were startled by a wonderful event. Enoch was translated, that he should not see death. Moses, the great earthly chronicler, tells us nothing of the manner of his translation, beyond this - he was not, for God took him. If the recording angel had been entering it in the chronicles of the Heavenly Kingdom, he would have written that He was, for God brought him up hither. Those simple, yet mysterious words, he was not, for God took him, seem written in anticipation of that coming mystery, when the world shall wonder because from the bed, or the mill, or the open field, one shall be taken, and the other shall be left.

We read that while Elijah still went on, and talked with Elisha, there appeared a chariot of fire and horses of fire, and parted them both asunder; and Elijah went up by a whirlwind into Heaven. God sent His carriage and pair for the prophet of Mount Carmel, who had done such mighty deeds; but Enoch, of whom nothing is recorded but that he walked with God, was honored on that heavenly journey with the company of God Himself. They were companions here on earth, and they went up together to the world of light and rest; and they walk together forevermore. Oh, dear friends, though we may be children of God, how much we shall lose if we sacrifice, for any earthly thing, that close intimacy with God in this world and through the ages of eternity!

Elijah thought that he was the only faithful man left in Israel; yet there was a whole school of the sons of the prophets who spent three days in seeking the body of their lost leader. And we may well suppose there were loving friends who sought for Enoch; but he was not found, for God had translated him. No man can suddenly disappear without being missed by someone. Let us so live that when we are removed from earth, we may be missed by many to whom in life we have been a blessing.

The brief record of Enoch's life presents him to us as a foreshadow of the Son of God on earth - alone, yet not alone, for the Father was with him. Enoch was alone, yet not alone, for he walked with God. And when he was translated, he changed his place, but not his company.

Enoch belonged to a long-lived family. Jared, Enoch's father, was the oldest man but one, being nine hundred and sixty-two years old at his death; and Methuselah, Enoch's son, lived to be nine hundred and sixty-nine years of age; but Enoch was taken away, or translated, in the very prime of life. We have this testimony concerning him in the Epistle to the Hebrews: By faith Enoch was translated that he should not see death; and was not found, because God had translated him; for before his translation he had this testimony, that he pleased God.

Now there is one thing we can settle in our minds distinctly: if he pleased God, he did not please men. It is impossible to do the two things. This world is at war with God; it has been for six thousand years, and will be as long as man is on the earth. We cannot please God and man. That which is highly esteemed by men is an abomination to God; and that which God esteems, men cast out as vile. Look at God's estimate of His Son; and of the Atonement that has been made. Man tramples it under his feet as if it were not worth having! Man rejects God's offer of mercy! There are men all around us who see no beauty in Christ; to whom He is as a root out of a dry ground, without form or comeliness. He is the richest jewel that Heaven ever had, and dearer to God than anything in Heaven or earth. When men are well pleased with and accept His Son, then it is that men and God agree.

What a testimony was that to Enoch! - he pleased God. Though men rejected his testimony, and did not like him because he went against the current of that day, it was everything to Enoch to know that he pleased God. I have heard some boys say, when they have been taunted by others, I don't care, I am pleasing my father; he is quite satisfied. If we can please God - that ought to be our aim in life. If we are living as we should be, we can please Him; and, if not, we certainly cannot please Him. Every one of us may follow Enoch. It is God's good pleasure that we should walk with Him, and have this testimony - that we are pleasing God.

Enoch was the first who was translated into the Kingdom of God without death. Each dispensation - the Patriarchal, the Legal, and the Gospel - had its representative in this respect in Enoch, Elijah, and Emmanuel. With regard to Enoch, we are simply told that he was not; at what time of the day or night we know not; for God took him. Elisha saw the chariot which conveyed Elijah to glory. And the little band of disciples who accompanied Him to Bethany were the spectators of Christ's ascension into Heaven, as your Representative and mine. He raised His wounded hands, and in the act of blessing He ascended. His voice grew fainter and fainter as He rose higher and higher, till a cloud received Him out of their sight. Who could we have to represent us to better advantage, in the Court of Heaven, than the Son with whom the Father is well pleased? If you have an advocate to attend to your case, you want him in the Court, do you not? That is the place for him. When Christ was here He was our Prophet; now He is our Priest; and when He comes again He will appear as our King. Enoch and Elijah are representing their dispensations; and we have this consolation, that we have our Representative.

How the thought that Enoch was thus the representative of that earliest dispensation ought to have brought the antediluvians into the dust before God! I believe, if they had taken Enoch's translation as a warning, and had turned from their sins to God, the Flood would never have destroyed the old world. I believe that we have not the faintest conception of the sin and iniquity which abounded in the days of Noah. Men had time to mature in every conceivable sin. Their guilt was so great that the Flood came and swept them all away. But Noah had no opportunity of seeing the wicked inhabitants swept from the face of the earth, as the window was so constructed that it looked towards the heavens. No one can imagine the blackness and wickedness of that day, the corruption and violence of the world, out of which Enoch was caught up.

What a translation it must have been! I think I see him going from mountain peak to mountain peak, rising higher and higher in his experience of God, until he became so heavenly-minded that God took him into His own presence. Away in the morning of history he found the highway of holiness, and walked in it. And if Enoch, in that dim light, in the early ages of the world, could walk with God, and have fellowship and communion with Him, how much more can we, who are living under the full blaze of Calvary, under the very shadow of the Cross of Jesus Christ!

Now, it is very evident that he lived for something outside of himself and outside of this world. He must have had a more powerful telescope than any now in use, notwithstanding the extraordinary improvements recently made in that instrument, for he could see into the very heavens; and he had his eye fixed upon the City which hath the foundations, whose Builder and Maker is God. By faith he could see, in that world of light, Him who is invisible. He was dead to the world. He had the world under his feet. He could see that everything was trifling here, and would soon pass away; - that even the earth itself would pass away, but that God's Kingdom was an everlasting Kingdom, and that He would reign forever; and he walked with God.

One day the cord that bound him to earth and time snapped asunder. God said unto him, Come up hither, and up he went to walk with Him in glory. God liked his company so well that He called His servant home. Dr. Andrew Bonar has said that Enoch took a long walk one day, and has not got back yet. With one bound he leaped the river of death, and walked the crystal pavement of Heaven - in the wilderness yesterday, in the promised land today.

Think of the society he was with on earth in the morning, and of that which he enjoyed in the evening! Think of what he was translated out of, and of what he entered into! Think of his being taken up out of this evil world, full of sin and iniquity, into the presence of the pure and holy God! Abel and Adam were there before him; and Jesus had not yet left the throne to come into the world and die, the Just for the unjust, that He might bring us to God. He saw Christ. Think of the ages He had been there, and the greatness of the reward Enoch had after walking with God only three hundred and sixty-five years! It was not long, after all, that he had to bear the scorn of men, compared with what he has enjoyed since. Think, too, of the reward that is set before us in yonder world if we are only true and faithful, and walk with God whilst we are on earth! Let us put the question to ourselves: Are we walking with God, like Enoch, or contrary to God? Every man was walking, in his day, towards the grave; but Enoch was entirely different. He had his heart and affections in another sphere. He was dead to the world. What charm had society for him? How many people now-a-days want a place in society - want to hold high positions even at the sacrifice of principle! They turn aside from the God of the Bible, and when they have attained to the goal of their ambition, that is the last we hear of them. But Enoch walked with God. When men get outside of themselves, their lives have an influence over other lives, and they live forever!

They walk with God whom none can shame
From trusting in His holy name:
Who looking for a glorious morn
Shrink not before the tip of scorn.
They walk in light, in safety, peace,
Awaiting patiently release;
Turn from the world and take the cross,
Even though it be of life the loss.
Thus Noah walked - an ark prepared
Thus moved by fear, salvation shared:
What, then, to him mans scoff and jeer?
God, the Almighty, was his fear.
So Abram walked when called to go
Forth to a land he did not know;
A stranger and a pilgrim here
Looked for a city to appear.
So Moses walked serene, endured
Affliction, and heavens rest secured:
And now the wealth of all the earth,
Compared with his, is little worth.
And thus God's heroes of all time,
So walk with Him in faith sublime;
The world is but a passage way
Through which they reach the realms of day.

- E. C. Pearson.

CHAPTER 9: LOT

ONE OBJECT I HAVE in presenting this character is to draw a contrast between a man who lived wholly for God, and was out-and-out a man of God and one who tried to live for both worlds: - or what we should consider a worldly professor of Christianity. We have such a contrast in the life of Daniel as contrasted with Lot.

Lot was one of those characters who are easily influenced. You may look upon his life as a failure, although in the sight of the world he would have been called in his day a success.

I think we have many more Lots nowadays than we have Daniel's. Where you can find one man like Daniel, Jeremiah, or John the Baptist, or Paul, you will find ten thousand men like Lot.

The first glimpse that we catch of this man was at Haran. He was a nephew of Abram, who was called the friend of God. God had called Abram out of his native land, away from the idolaters that surrounded him, into the promised land, and we are told that Lot, his nephew, went with him. And I think, perhaps, that is just the key to his character. He went with Abram. So long as he stayed with Abram he got on very well. His mistake was in leaving him. Some men all through life have to be bolstered up by others. When they are at home, home has an influence over them; or while they are among their relatives or friends they stand well, but when they are away, and trial and temptation come, and the world comes in like a flood upon them, they are carried away.

The Scriptural account we have of Lot is in Genesis 11. In verse 31 we are told that "Terah took Abram his son, and Lot the son of Haran, his sons son, and Sarai his daughter-in-law, his son Abrams wife; and they went forth with them from Ur of the Chaldees, to go into the land of Canaan, and they came unto Haran and dwelt there."

Abram and Lot were at Haran for five years. Haran was halfway between the land that Abram was called from and the land that he was called to. He only came halfway out. I think a good many men have got to Haran, and there they remain. They are not more than half converted. They want to live on the borders all the while. They neither enjoy the world nor Christ. They have enough religion to make them wretched, but not enough to make them joyful. They need some calamity to bring them completely out of the world. So it was with Abram and Lot.

They stayed there until Abrams father died. It has been quaintly said - We never get beyond the half-way house until our old man is dead. After this

Abram moved into the promised land, where his faith was tested. When he arrived he found the country inhabited; and he had not been there very long when a famine struck the land. Then Abram took his nephew, Lot, and went down into Egypt, where they were successful from a worldly point of view. They grew rich; but when riches come troubles generally come with them. When they came out of Egypt into the promised land there was a strife among the herdsmen of Abram and of Lot. They got into a quarrel. But no one could have a lawsuit with Abram. He said to his young nephew, "Now we cannot afford to quarrel here before these heathen - before the nations around us; we must set them a good example. And now you take the right or you take the left, and let there be no strife among our men." He let Lot choose - and Lots choice was a terrible mistake.

Wealth becomes a trouble if it is procured in Haran, or Egypt, or Sodom. It brings no blessing if God's people get it out of Canaan. It was in Egypt that Abram denied his wife. God did not call Abram there, but to the promised land where his faith had to be tried; and where he stayed but a little while, before he went down to Egypt to escape the famine. There he got riches, and sorrow with them; as we read: And Lot also, which went with Abram, had flocks, and herds, and tents. And the land was not able to bear them, that they might dwell together: for their substance was great, so that they could not dwell together. And there was a strife between the herdsmen of Abrams cattle and the herdsmen of Lots cattle: and the Canaanite and the Perizzite dwelled then in the land. And Abram said unto Lot, Let there be no strife, I pray thee, between me and thee, and between my herdsmen and thy herdsmen; for we be brethren. Is not the whole land before thee? separate thyself, I pray thee, from me: if thou wilt take the left hand, then I will go to the right; of if thou depart to the right hand, then I will go to the left.

"And Lot lifted up his eyes, and beheld all the plain of Jordan, that it was well watered everywhere, before the Lord destroyed Sodom and Gomorrah, even as the Garden of the Lord, like the land of Egypt, as thou comest unto Zoar. Then Lot chose him all the plain of Jordan; and Lot journeyed east: and they separated themselves the one from the other. Abram dwelled in the land of Canaan, and Lot dwelled in the cities of the plain, and pitched his tent toward Sodom. But the men of Sodom were wicked and sinners before the Lord exceedingly. Lot allowed the world to get the advantage; and that is where thousands of Christians are failing in the present day. They do not let the Lord choose for them in regard to temporal things, and they make great mistakes."

Lot never ought to have left Abram. If he had lost some of his property, if he had not got on quite so well, if he had not accumulated wealth quite so fast, it would have been better for him and his family - if he had never left that holy man whom the Lord delighted to talk with, that man who was in communion with God, and to whom the angels often came, and brought messages from Heaven. But Lot was probably like a great many men around us. He was careless; he was covetous; he looked to the right and he looked to the left, and he looked toward Sodom, and observed the well-watered plains, I imagine him saying, Now, if I take these well-watered plains, I can accumulate wealth very fast. I know Sodom is a very wicked place, but I will not go to Sodom. He at first did not intend to go into Sodom; but he had pitched his tent toward Sodom; and when a man begins to pitch his tent toward Sodom, and to look at it, it will not be long before he will be inside. His heart will be there, and by and by his heart will take him down to Sodom. Lot does it to sell cattle. He goes down to Sodom to transact business, and some of the business men tell him that he would succeed much better in Sodom than he could living out there on the plain, and he had better come down into the city.

He knew it was an exceedingly wicked place. He knew that there were very great sinners there. He knew it was corrupt. He knew there was danger of his being ruined; and if he had only looked into the future, and could have seen that it would be ruin to his family, he would not have put his children right into the way of temptation. But he took them down into that city. He left the society of Abram, and went into Sodom. There was his mistake. He did not let God choose for him.

I most firmly believe that more men make a mistake just there than in any other situation in life. Many a man starts out, and he does not ask God to direct him in his business or his plans. If Lot had asked the God of Abram to have selected for him and guided him, He would never have led him to Sodom. God knew what was going to take place there. He knew that judgment was coming down on those cities of the plain.

But Lot was like a great many men nowadays. He thought that he could manage his own affairs. He did not want God to interfere with his business transactions. He could pray about spiritual things, but he did not think it necessary to pray about his business. The idea that he should ask God when he had such a chance as that! He could have all these well-watered plains, and he chose them.

Now, after Lot had been in Sodom for a little while, and had become known to the men of Sodom, you would probably have found them saying he was very successful, and that he would be a much richer man than his uncle Abram in a little while. He was a long-sighted man. As a friend said the other day, Lot was considered a very long-sighted man in the eyes of the world, and Abram just the reverse; but which had the longest sight in the end? Abram had got a glimpse of the city which hath the foundations, whose Builder and Maker is God. He lived for another world; he did not live for this. He was the long-sighted man, and Lot was the short-sighted one. And these men whom we now call farseeing, whom we call so shrewd and so wise, oh, how many of them are blind!

Lot was one of those men who are determined to die rich. There was a man taken into one of our insane asylums a few years ago, from one of the Western cities; he was resolved to be rich. I was acquainted with him. How he just turned every stone to accumulate wealth! All his energy and every faculty was pushed toward that one end. Wealth, wealth, wealth! money, money,

money! was his cry, and at last it drove him mad, and they took him to the madhouse, where he threw himself into a rocking-chair, and cried, Millions of money, and in a madhouse! That was all there was of his life. Pretty short, wasn't it? Sixty years gone, millions of money, and in a madhouse; and he died there. That was the summing up of his life.

There is many a man determined to be rich, though he has to take his children into temptation. I cannot conceive of a greater calamity that can happen any mans child than to have all the money he wants to spend, and nothing to do. And this was the drift of Lots family.

But yet he was not without warning.

War came on, and the Kings of Sodom and Gomorrah were defeated, and the enemy took Lot, and all his property, with spoil from both the cities, and fled. A messenger came and told Abram; when he heard of it he took his trained servants and started in pursuit of the enemy; he overtook them, defeated them in battle, rescued the prisoners, and brought back their goods.

Melchizedek, the King of Salem and priest of the Most High God, came forth with bread and wine, and blessed Abram. Then the King of Sodom came out and said to him, Now, you may still have the money; you may take the goods; but give me the souls. But a man that has been blessed by Melchizedek, who is first by interpretation King of Righteousness, and after that also King of Salem, which is King of Peace, is not to be tempted by the goods of Sodom. Abram says, I have lifted up my hand to the God of Heaven and earth, that I will not take a thing from the King of Sodom. It should not be said that the King of Sodom had made Abram rich. He did not want any Sodom money, for if he took Sodom money he would have to take Sodom judgment when that judgment came. Now, instead of Lot staying out of Sodom, as he ought to have done, he went back into it. I can imagine him saying: I must go back and make up what I have lost. There was another of Lots mistakes - returning to the city after such a warning as he had had. But he went back; and from that day until destruction came upon Sodom - final destruction - and the city was destroyed, Lot was perhaps the most popular man in it.

He was popular because he was the nephew of the man who had been such a benefactor to the men of Sodom; and if you had gone into the city a few years after, you would have found him one of the most successful and one of the shrewdest and keenest men in all the cities of the plain, in the sight of the men of Sodom.

They would have told you how he came off the plains only a few years before, worth only a few thousand dollars, and now he had accumulated great wealth. You would have found his name among the very highest in the social list. His family moved in the upper ten, in the highest circles as far as the world was concerned. He got into office. We find him sitting in the gate, which was a sign that he held the office of judge or other high position.

He was a very honorable man in the eyes of the men of Sodom. He had got into the society of kings and princes, and in the eyes of the world was a very prosperous man. He may have had a title to his name - The Hon. John C. Lot, of Sodom, would sound very well. And he was perhaps a very prominent candidate for political honors, and they all desired to show him respect because he was wealthy. Perhaps he owned the very best corner lots in Sodom; and if they had the custom of putting their names on buildings as they do now, you would have found Lot on a great many of the finest buildings in Sodom. Yes, getting on amazingly well. And if he was a judge, Judge Lot would have sounded well, would it not? If they had had railroads then, he would have been one of the most prominent men in all those movements; he would have had large shares in the railroads, and been to the front in all stock operations. He was one of those men who had not religion enough, as the world says, to make him unpopular. He was a man of immense influence. That is what they would have told you down in Sodom. There was not a man in the whole city who had more influence than Lot.

The world thought that Abram had made a great mistake, He stayed out there on the plains with his tent and altar, and if he came to Sodom when Lot did, he too might have had a high position. You would have found Mrs. Lot driving, perhaps, four-in-hand, the best turn-out in Sodom, and her daughters at the theaters, and in most places of amusement, and there is the family, just moving in the very highest circles in that city.

That is what the world calls prosperity. That is what they call getting on. And you would have found, probably, that Lot was reported to be the richest man in all Sodom, and if they had to pay income tax, then his would have stood the highest; a shrewd man, a wise man, a successful man. That is the man of the world.

He is the successful man. But, look! Though everything was moving on well, when he had been there twenty years, this wise man, this influential man, had not won a convert. These worldly Christians don't get many converts - note that. These men who are so very influential seldom get many converts to Christ. The world goes stumbling over them. Lot was what we might call a paying, but not a praying member. Some men seem to boast of that, and they will tell you with a good deal of pride. Well I am one of the paying members; and when they come into church they have the very best pew, and they come swinging down the broad aisle, and the whole church turns round to look at them: they say, "He is one of the best men we have - one of the most liberal men in the congregation; it is true he seldom comes out to the prayer meetings, for he is not a praying man." You will not find him identifying himself with the despised, and taking a stand among the poor and helping them; that was not the character of Lot.

At last two messengers appear at the gate of the city. The sun is setting on Sodom for the last time. The men of the City would see it in the morning when it would rise; but it was never going to set on those five cities of the plain again. And when the messengers - for there was not any written word then as now; God often sent His messages by angels in that dispensation, who held communion with men - when these messengers arrived at the gate, it seems they meet Lot there, and Lot knew them. But it had been probably a long time since he had seen any messengers of that kind. When he lived back there on the plain with Abram, it was quite a common thing for Abram to entertain angels; they brought many a sweet communication from Heaven to him. But now they come down to see what Lot is doing, and what a miserable, shocking state of things they see! Here was the nephew of that sainted man of God immersed in Sodom, and his family, you might say, wrecked and ruined. And Lot got up and bowed and asked them to his house; but they refused to go into his house. They said, No, we will walk about the streets tonight; we have come to take account of this city. But he constrained them, and they went in; and when it was noised through Sodom that he was entertaining two men, it was not long before his house was surrounded by a great crowd. An awful scene ensued. When the men of Sodom came and demanded of Lot to send those men out, he came outside of his house and closed the door, and besought them, begged them, not to harm them. Now see how much influence he has got. This fellow came in to sojourn, and he will needs be a judge. And they pressed sore upon him, and almost burst in the door; and if the messengers had not come out and smitten the crowd with blindness, they would have slain Lot right there. They had not the least respect for him.

The world is just now cheering on some of these worldly professors, and talking about their being men of great position and great influence. But the world cares not for you. If you make one false step, how they will sneer; if misfortune comes upon you and you lose your property, then you will see how much they respect you. How much did they care for Lot? He had such great influence and such high position, but it is all gone now.

The angels said to him, "Hast thou anywhere besides, any of your family here?" And what did they find? Why, his children; his daughters had married men of Sodom. Oh, what a fall! You take your children to Sodom, and you will find it will not be long before they will want to stay there. It is easier to lead your children into temptation than it is to lead them out. What a mistake Lot had made! He had taken them away from the society of Sarah and Abram, that holy family, living out on the plain in communion with Heaven daily. He had taken them down to Sodom, and they were steeped in the sins of Sodom. The angels said to him, If you have any here beside, go in haste and bring them out. And you can see that old man with his gray hairs and his head bowed down, moving heart-broken through the streets of Sodom, at the midnight hour. All that he had accumulated was going to be swept away now. God was going to destroy the city. Lot, make haste; get your family out of this place. Look at him. He goes to a house, and you can hear him knocking at the dead hour of night. At last someone gets up and opens the window, and puts his head out. "Who is there?" "It is your father-in-law, Lot." "Well, what are you here at this time of night for?" "I have a couple of messengers at my house; they have come down from Heaven to tell me that God is going to destroy this place, and He wants to have me get you out; come to my house at once, that we may leave the city early in the morning."

But they mock him. Ah! poor Lot has lost his testimony; we never hear that he had put up an altar in Sodom; his own children do not believe him; they mock him. I tell you, when men live so like the world that their own children have no confidence in their piety, they have sunk very low. When a man cannot influence his own children, even though he has made millions, what a wreck he has made of life! You talk about a man being successful. You must trace him from the cradle to the grave to see how successful he is. You want to see what influence he leaves behind him; you want to see how he leaves his family: and then you can judge whether a man is successful or not. For a man to accumulate wealth, and ruin his family and leave a blight upon them, that is not true success.

Thus the old man at the midnight hour is pleading with his children to come with him. But they mock him. Why, Sodom was never more prosperous than now. There is no sign of a coming judgment; no sign that Sodom is going to be burnt up.

The Savior tells us they were eating and drinking, buying and selling, planting and building; all went on as usual. They did not believe there was any sign of the coming judgment. The sun shone as brightly the day before their destruction as it had shone for years. The stars then, perhaps were glittering in the heavens as brightly as ever; and the moon threw her light down upon the city; and Lot's sons-in-law mocked him. He coudn't get them out. I see him going through the streets with his head bowed down and great tears trickling down his cheeks. Ask him now about his life, and he will tell you it has been a total failure. He goes back to his home; and early in the morning the angels had to take him almost by force and hasten him out of the city. He could not bear the thought of leaving his loved ones there to perish while God dealt in judgment with that city.

My friends, is not that a fair picture of hundreds and thousands at the present time? Have you not been trying to accumulate wealth even to the neglect of your children, so that today they are lifting up their voices against your God, and against your Bible, and against you? They do not care for your feelings; are they not trampling them under their feet? Perhaps many of the parents have gone to their graves, and the children are now squandering what their parents gathered together.

What an example we have here in the case of Lot, and how it ought to open the eyes of many a business man, and cause him to see that his life is going to be a total wreck if he takes his children into Sodom's judgment when the judgment comes.

Away yonder on the plain of Mamre, I see Abraham standing before the Lord, and pleading, pleading, pleading, that the righteous may not perish with the wicked. But God is more pitiful than even Abrahams prayer. Not only will He save the righteous, but He will spare the city if He can find fifty righteous there. But Abraham doubts if there be so many. Peradventure there are forty, wilt Thou destroy the city for lack of ten? No; if there are forty; or thirty, yes, or twenty, or even ten, I will spare Sodom for their sake. Now, thinks Abraham, surely Lot and his household and family are safe. Surely even down in Sodom there is a church in his house, at least ten souls. Alas! no, Abraham! Not a solitary one except Lot himself. They had all become infected with the moral disease of Sodom - pride, fullness of bread and abundance of idleness; this was her iniquity; neither did she strengthen the poor and needy; and they were haughty and committed abomination before God; therefore He destroyed them as He saw good. But it shall be more tolerable in the day of judgment for Sodom and Gomorrah than for those who in these enlightened days have walked in the same evil ways.

THE END OF A BACKSLIDER

Now, just take an inventory of what that man lost. He lost twenty years of time. We do not find that he did any good down there at all; he did not get one inhabitant out of the doomed city. These worldly Christians that talk about having an influence over the world - where is it? I would like to see it. Will you tell me where there is a worldly Christian who has tarried in the race in order to save men; where are the men he has reached? Not one man won to God in all those twenty years by Lot. He lost all his property; everything he gained in Sodom - he lost it all; he lost his family all but his two daughters, and they were so stained by the sins of Sodom that they soon fell into an awful sin; and the last thing we see of Lot is on the mountain side, where he has fallen into that sin and become the father of the Moabites and the Ammonites that ever afterwards were the enemies of God and His people. What a dark picture it is, the end of a poor backslider; the end of a man that went to Sodom and lived for Sodom, and had to take Sodom's judgment.

Ah, my friends, what a contrast between the end of Lot and the end of Daniel, or of Elijah, or John the Baptist, or any of those men who stood true to God. How their names shine now upon the pages of history and how their light comes down through the centuries! But look at Lot. What a wreck!

And yet that is the man whom the world calls successful while he is living. Ah, there is many a man today who is just following the footsteps of Lot, seeking to get wealth, seeking to get position in this world, setting aside the God of Abraham, setting aside the God of the Bible, and trampling the prayers of their mothers and fathers under their feet. They say Give me wealth and I will give you everything else. Shall we not learn the lesson? Shall we not profit by the life of Lot? I believe that is what these lives are recorded for.

Father, let me ask this question. Where are your sons? Where are your children? Let the question come home to you – where are they? And if they have gone astray, who is to blame? Who is to blame?

I heard not long ago of a young man who came home a number of times drunk, and the servants told the father of it. He said: Well, I will sit up tonight and will see. He sat up until past midnight, and then he heard someone trying to get the latch-key into the door. He listened and listened. It was a long time before the young man entered. The father went and stood in the hall, and when his boy came in he saw that he was drunk. Immediately he ordered him out of the house. He said, Never show yourself here again; I will not have you coming to my house and disgracing me. But after the son had been gone a little while the father could not sleep; he remembered that he was the first one that put temptation in the way of the boy, for he had had liquor upon his own table. Well now, I am to blame, he said. And he got out of bed and dressed himself, and went out upon the streets and asked a policeman if he had seen the young man. After hunting for hours, at last he found his drunken son, and brought him home; and when he became sober he said, My son, I am more to blame than you are. He wept over him, and asked his boy to forgive him, and he said, Now let us try to lead different lives. And the father set his son a better example, and saved him from destruction.

There is many a man who has ruined his own sons; who has taken them into the way of temptation and they have gone astray. May God show us, as fathers, the importance of living rightly before our children; and if we are doing anything in any business that is dishonorable, in order to make money for our children, better a thousand times for us to leave them a clean record, a clean character, than to leave them millions of money that we have not got honestly. I tell you we need to have children a good deal shrewder and wiser than we have at the present time, to keep the money that has been gathered dishonestly. It is a good deal better to live with God and leave them less, and leave them a good, clean character, such as Daniel left in Babylon, than it is to take them down to Sodom and live as Lot did, and have judgment come upon them, after we were dead and gone.

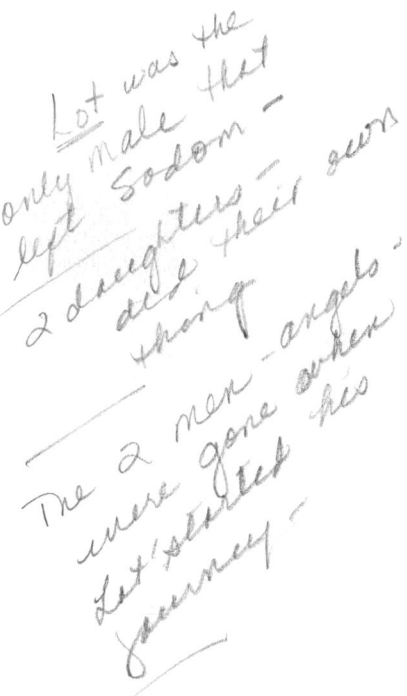

CHAPTER 10: JACOB

IN CALLING ATTENTION to the Life and Character of Jacob, my object is to help young disciples to study the Bible.

One of the greatest mistakes made by people who attempt to study the Word of God is that they have no system about it. They take up the Bible, and read a chapter here and a chapter there, and then take a glimpse of a mans life, perhaps the beginning of it, or the middle, or the close, and they are all the time getting into darkness and trouble, and say they do not understand the Word of God. Now, one way to read and study the Bible is to take up the life of one of these characters, because if it were not important that we should read the whole life the Holy Ghost would not have had it recorded. It has been recorded for our profit; and if we take up the Bible and read a part of a mans life, and do not follow it out, we shall not understand it. The way to read the Epistles is to read a whole Epistle at once. If you have only time to read a chapter or two, go to the Psalms or Proverbs. But you cannot understand much about the Book of Ruth, or the Book of Esther, for instance, by reading one chapter. You must read the whole book to understand it.

One chapter that Paul wrote to the Corinthians cannot be understood unless you read the whole Epistle. If I write a letter, and the person receiving it takes out the middle of it, and does not read the beginning nor the end, and then complains that he did not understand it, there would be no one to blame but himself. And that is being done constantly with the Word of God.

Perhaps there is no character of the whole Bible, unless it is David, that people stumble over more than the character of Jacob; they say that a great many things that Jacob did were wrong, and that God sanctioned them. That is a mistake which is being constantly made. If they would take the whole life of Jacob, the beginning and the end, and read it through carefully, they would find how God dealt with Jacob, and how He punished him according to his ways. And you will find that Hosea gives us the key to Jacobs character and to his life: "The Lord hath also a controversy with Judah, and will punish Jacob according to his ways; according to his doings will he recompense him." As you read his life you will find that idea running all through it. God will punish Jacob according to his ways, and according to his doings will He recompense him.

Jacob was a man who always had an eye to his own advantage. He always wanted an agreement, so that he might get the best of it. But very often people of this kind do not get on any better than others. We see this in the parable of the laborers sent by the householder into his vineyard: For the kingdom of

Heaven is like unto a man that is a householder, which went out early in the morning to hire laborers into his vineyard. And when he had agreed with the laborers for a penny a day, he sent them into his vineyard. And he went out about the third hour, and saw others standing idle in the market place, and said unto them, Go ye also into the vineyard, and whatsoever is right I will give you. And they went their way. Again he went out about the sixth and ninth hour and did likewise. And about the eleventh hour he went out and found others standing idle, and said unto them, Why stand ye here all the day idle? They say unto him, Because no man hath hired us. He saith unto them, Go ye also into the vineyard; and whatsoever is right, that shall ye receive.

Now when the evening was come, and this man was going to settle with his servants, he gave orders that those hired last should come first, and he gave them each a penny, and to those that went at the ninth hour and sixth hour he gave a penny. And those that he hired first, when they came, only received a penny. Then these began to complain about the good man, and to say bitter things against him. Sometimes when you have been traveling, and when you have hired a cab, and have paid the lawful fare, the driver takes the money, and looks at it and then at you, as if you were treating him very shabbily. And when you speak to him about it, and ask him if you have not paid him the lawful fare, he is obliged to confess that you have. So, when the householder came to pay the men that had been working in the heat of the day, they complained, and he said, Didn't you agree? Those that he hired first made a bargain. They would not go out in the vineyard and work until they had made a bargain. They wanted to know how much they were to get. Now, mark this, wherever you find professed children of God, who are all the time making bargains with the Lord, or wanting to, you will find they come out poorest after all. Those other men went to the vineyard. They trusted the good man of the vineyard, and they got on a good deal better than the men who made a bargain. So the good man said, Did you not agree with me? Was it not a bargain? Jacob was one of the men who are always making a bargain. He could trust the Lord as far as he could see Him, and no further. He was one of these earthly-minded saints, who are all the time walking by sight and not by faith. And if you want to get a sharp contrast between two men, take Jacob, and then take his son Joseph. One walked by sight, and the other by faith. If Jacob had had to go through the trials that Joseph had, he would have complained, and thought his journey had been a very hard one. And yet how much better Joseph got on than Jacob!

I believe that the lives of these men have been recorded for our profit: not that we may, as some people do, hide behind them and say that God justified their sin; but that you and I might profit by their mistakes, and not fall into them ourselves.

There was a young minister who took a church in Scotland, and he began to preach about the sins of the present day, and those of the people who came to hear him. The old sexton, came to him and said, "Young man, if you expect to hold this people you must be careful about preaching on modern sins. You can preach about the sins of Abraham, and Isaac, and Jacob, and the old Patriarchs, but don't you preach about the sins of the present day, because the people will not stand it."

Now, I do not want to fall into that error. Do not think I am bringing up the life of Jacob and his failings, that it may ease our consciences and justify ourselves. But I want we should remember that many of us are very much like Jacob. Where you will find one Joseph now, and one Daniel, and Joshua, you will find five thousand Jacobs. The church is full of Jacobs at the present time; and a great many people seem to think they get on better if they are worldly-minded. They think it is a sign of prosperity if they can only secure the good things of earth, and yet get to Heaven. That is about as high as most people get. They just barely get to Heaven, and that is all. But they want to have a good time down here upon earth, and make the most of this world.

I am afraid that Jacob started out with something of that idea, and he had a rough journey - a perilous voyage. It is a good deal better to be out and out for God, and to walk by faith, than it is to walk by sight, and be all the time making bargains with the Lord.

Now, his name means - a deceiver, a supplanter. The beginning of the trouble was perhaps with the father and mother. We are told that Rebekah loved Jacob, and Isaac loved Esau; where there is partiality in any family there is always trouble. Rebekah planned to keep Jacob at home and to get Esau out; she took it out of the hands of the Lord and began to plan herself. And the result was that Jacob, whom she loved, left, and she did not live to see him return. Thus she failed in the very thing she wanted to accomplish.

"And Jacob went out from Beersheba, and went toward Haran. And he lighted upon a certain place, and tarried there all night, because the sun was set; and he took of the stones of that place, and put them for his pillow, and lay down in that place to sleep. And he dreamed; and behold, a ladder set up on the earth, and the top of it reached to Heaven; and behold, the angels of God ascending and descending on it.

"And behold, the Lord stood above it, and said, I am the Lord God of Abraham, thy father, and the God of Isaac; the land whereon thou liest, to thee will I give it, and to thy seed. And thy seed shall be as the dust of the earth; and thou shalt spread abroad to the west, and the east, and to the north, and to the south; and in thee and thy seed shall all the families of the earth be blessed. And behold, I am with thee, and will keep thee in all places whither thou goest, and will bring thee again into this land; for I will not leave thee until I have done that which I have spoken to thee of. And Jacob awaked out of his sleep, and he said, Surely the Lord is in this place; and I knew it not. And he was afraid, and said, How dreadful is this place! This is none other but the house of God, and this is the gate to Heaven."

We very often hear that quoted in our meetings. Men come into the church and say, "This is the house of God, and this is the gate of Heaven;" and when people come into the house of God they put on a sober appearance, and they act as if there was something very strange about the house of God, as if it was the gate of Heaven.

Now, I would not say a word to detract from the holiness of the house of God. But let us bear in mind that every place ought to be holy to a man of God; that in every place we ought to be true to God. We ought to be as true to Him in our place of business as we are in the house of God; and when Jacob said, This is the house of God, and this is the gate of Heaven, he was under the canopy of high Heaven. That was where God met him; and God will meet us in the street as well as in a place of worship. He will meet us at home.

People come together, and say that where two or three are met in His name, there will He be in the midst of them. But He is also with us in our closets. We are told in another place to go into our closets and shut the door. Any place where God is is holy, and this putting on another air and a sanctimonious look when we come into the house of God, and laying it aside when we go out, and falling into sin again, thinking that it is going to be acceptable to God if we go to church every Sabbath, is all wrong. Every place ought to be holy to a true child of God.

"And Jacob rose up early in the morning, and took the stone that he had put for his pillows, and set it up for a pillar, and poured oil upon the top of it. And he called the name of that place Bethel; but the name of that city was called Luz at first. And Jacob vowed a vow, saying, If God will be with me, and will keep me in this way that I go, and will give me bread to eat, and raiment to put on, so that I come again to my fathers house in peace; then shall the Lord be my God."

This is Jacobs response to the promise God made from the top of that ladder. He said that He would be with him; that He would make his seed like the dust of the earth; that He would never leave him; that He would bless him, and that He would bring him back again, and that He would give him a good title to all that land; that the whole country should be his and belong to his posterity: and Jacob answers, "Now, Lord if Thou wilt give me enough to eat, and enough to drink, and enough to wear, so that I come again to my fathers house, then Thou shalt be my God."

You see he was making a bargain. Instead of being content with that glorious covenant which God had just made with him, and entering into that promised land, and taking God at His word, and thanking God for what He had done, he gets up and puts that if in. If Thou wilt give me enough, and bring me home safe, then Thou shalt be my God. He wanted to make a bargain right there with the Lord, the first thing he did after the God of all grace had met him and spoken to him such wonderful things, and told him how He would bless him and exalt him to Heaven. Think of this great privilege! Yet he could not see anything beyond this life. He was really world-minded, and could not rise into the high state that God wanted him to.

Now, we find that he goes down to Haran, and stays there twenty years. Take note, he had gone away with a lie on his lips, and he goes to his uncles, and begins to make sharp bargains. But any man who has been to Bethel and got his conscience quickened is no match for the world; and Jacob got cheated every time. He worked seven years for his wife, and then he got deceived, and another woman was married to him; and then he has to work seven years longer for the woman he wanted. You see he was paid back in his own coin. He lied to his aged father; and now his uncle is lying to him. He deceived his father; and now he is being deceived: and instead of working seven years for Rachel he worked fourteen, and his wages were changed ten different times. After being there twenty long years, if you will read his life carefully, you will find that he did not make anyone much better, nor had he much influence over his uncle Laban.

After meeting God at Bethel and receiving such a promise, he could have afforded to be very generous - he could have afforded to leave himself in God's hands and let God plan for him; but instead of that he begins to plan for himself, and he was trying to drive sharp bargains with Laban, and he got cheated every time. You do not hear of his having an altar there, or of his giving one-tenth of his goods; but, after he had been there twenty long years, one day the God of Abraham appeared to him and said: "I am the God of Bethel, where thou anointed the pillar, and where thou vowed a vow unto Me: now arise, get thee out from this land, and return unto the land of thy kindred."

God had not neglected His promise, nor broken His vow. If God was as forgetful as you and I are, I do not know what would become of us. Think of all the vows you have made; think of all the promises that you have made before God, and broken. Have you never promised God that you would love Him and serve Him, and become His child? Have you never promised a dying mother, or a dying child, or some loved friend, at the dying hour, that you would turn your face toward Heaven and live for God? - and ten, fifteen or twenty years have passed, and that vow is still unkept: it is a broken vow! For twenty long years Jacob seemed to have forgotten all about his vow at Bethel, but God made him the promise, and it was an unconditional one; and now God comes to him and says, "I am the God of Bethel; I am the God that met you at Bethel; arise, and leave this country, and go back to your own home."

Now see how Jacob begins to plan. He had now a commission from high Heaven to go. If he had been like Joshua he would have walked right out with his head up; but instead of that he begins to plan how he could escape; and he stole away like a coward. While his uncle was absent, Jacob took his servants and all his cattle and his wives, and fled as if he were guilty of some great crime. His father-in-law, when he heard of it, marshaled his servants together and went after him; but while he was fleeing away God interfered, and said to Laban the night before he overtook Jacob, Say nothing to him of it, either good or bad. God was going to protect him; God was going to keep His word; He had promised to do it, and Laban could not touch him; God would not allow him to do so. And they met the next day, and Laban did what the God of Abraham told him to do, and they parted friends. After that difficulty had been settled, and Jacob had done right, and what God had told him to do, then the angels came out to escort him back, and he said, Is not this God's host? But instead of going right back, as God told him to do, he began to plan again to meet Esau. You see he is all the time planning, planning, planning. There are a great many Christians of this kind now-a-days. They take themselves out of the hands of the Lord, and are all the time planning for themselves. Jacob then did a very mean, contemptible thing. He took the wife that he did not love very much, and some of his cattle, and sent them on before, thinking if Esau should come out to slay them that he would escape: It was a mean, cowardly act.

But now God appears to him. After they had passed over one evening, and the hour was soon coming when he was to meet Esau, who threatened his life, he was alone, and the God of Bethel met him again. See what took place: And Jacob was left alone; and there wrestled a man with him until the breaking of the day. Now mark what it says: There wrestled a man with him until the breaking of the day. It is thought by many that the Jehovah of the Old Testament is the Jesus of the New.

"And when He saw that He prevailed not against him, He touched the hollow of his thigh; and the hollow of Jacobs thigh was out of joint, as he wrestled with Him. And He said, Let me go, for the day breaketh. And he said, I will not let Thee go, except Thou bless me. And He said unto him, What is thy name? And he said, Jacob. And He said, Thy name shall be called no more Jacob, but Israel; for as a prince hast thou power with God and with men, and hast prevailed."

Now, when did he have the power? When did he prevail? Why, it was when his thigh was out of joint that he prevailed. Now, a man whose thigh is out of joint cannot wrestle much; he is very weak, an a little child can throw him down then; and when we have not strength, all we can do is to hold on, and then the blessing will come. And these men who are trying to work by the energy of the flesh, and to wrestle with God, and to force a blessing out of His hands, have a false idea of God entirely. God stands with His arms full of blessings. His hands are outstretched to the sinner, and He says, Here they are; take them. All this fighting is with mans own self. The Scripture says, Strive to enter in at the strait gate. Who are we to strive with? Not with the gate-keeper. The gate-keeper stands with the gate wide open, and he says, Come in, come in. But all the striving is with the flesh; it is with this old carnal nature of ours. When Jacob was weak, then he was strong, and then he prevailed; as a prince he had power with God.

"And Jacob asked Him, and said, Tell me, I pray Thee, Thy name. And He said, Wherefore is it that thou dost ask after My name? And He blessed him there. And Jacob called the name of the place Peniel: for I have seen God face to face; and my life is preserved."

Now, we might have thought that he would have been altogether different from that hour; and some people tell us that he was; I suppose he was, because the Lord blessed him, and that is a pretty good sign: but I think as you read on through his life, you will find that he had not got complete victory over himself, because the next thing you hear is that he is at Shechem, and he builds an altar there, and he calls it El-elohe-Israel. There are a good many men down at Shechem now who have got altars there; they have got a religion, and will tell you that they would not give it up for all the world: but when a man tells you that he would not give up his religion, you may know that he has not much religion to give up. When a man begins to stand up for my religion, as you very often hear, you may know there is something wrong. That is not what we want. We want them to change their lives, and a religion that does not save men from sin is not worth going across the street after. A religion of that kind is a mere empty form, and worthless. Jacob got to Shechem, and he built an altar there.

"God said unto Jacob, Arise, go up to Bethel, and dwell there; and make there an altar unto God, that appeared unto thee when thou fleddest from the face of Esau thy brother. Then Jacob said unto his household, and to all that were with him, Put away the strange gods that are among you, and be clean, and change your garments."

You see, while he was at Shechem he had built an altar, and had got a lot of strange gods, too. Now, from the beginning of creation to the present time you will find that one of the things the God of the Bible will never allow is, that any god should be put before Him; and yet here was Jacob, whom God had met at Bethel and blessed, now at Shechem, surrounded by a lot of idols. And I think that is the weakness of the church today. When there was no strange god - it says in one place in the Scripture - when there was no strange god with Jacob, God made him ride on the high places of the earth; and so I believe the weakness of the church today lies in the fact that we have these strange gods in our midst. We need not go to Japan, or to China, or to India, to find people with idols. I will venture to say we have not got to go a mile to find them. They may not bow down to the gods of Egypt, the gods of iron, stone and wood, that they have made with their own hands; but anything that comes between me and the God of Heaven is an idol; anything that disturbs my communion with God is an idol. And I will venture to say there is many a professed child of God today who makes an idol of the card-table, who makes an idol of novels, of dancing, of the theater, of fashion, of self, of pleasure, of money. There are many who bow down to the golden calf today; and the reason why there is so little power in the church of God today is that we have got too many idols.

Now God says to Jacob, "Arise, go up to Bethel." And the first thing he did was to put away his strange gods. He knew he was going to meet God in Bethel, and that he could not have his idols before Him; that they had to be put away - that was the first thing; and they dug a grave there under the oak at Shechem, and they brought their idols and put them in, and buried them in that grave. I wish that a great grave were dug, so that we might take every one of our idols and roll them into it. What a blessing it would be! How the fear of God would fall upon the people! And men who are living in sin and rejoicing over their sins, and who are not ashamed to confess their sins in the street, or in their places of business, who are not ashamed to own that they are enemies of the gospel of Jesus Christ - those very men would begin to tremble. We never see the church putting away its idols and cleansing itself of its sins, but that the world will begin to inquire what they shall do to be saved.

We are living in an age of formalism. "In the last days perilous times shall come; for men shall be lovers of their own selves, covetous, boasters, proud, blasphemers... without natural affection... having a form of godliness, but denying the power thereof."

Let us be careful that we are not simply empty professors. Let us see that we do not scheme, and build altars, saying, This is my church; this is my religion; this is my doctrine; this is my creed. Let us see that we have Christ in the heart; that is the main thing. A man may be very religious, and have no Christ. The world is full of religion. Religion is one thing, Christ is another. Let us see where we are. How many professed Christians there are who have gone to Shechem; they have moved down there and taken all their family; they have an altar there; and because it is fashionable they go to church on Sunday morning; they like to get into society and have their sons and daughters do the same, and, therefore, they go to church; but many of them are in the same condition that Jacob was at Shechem, with an altar, and at the same time with idols right in their own houses. After he had put away his idols he says:

"Let us arise, and go up to Bethel; and I will make there an altar unto God, who answered me in the day of my distress, and was with me in the way which I went. And they gave unto Jacob all the strange gods which were in their hand, and all their earrings which were in their ears; and Jacob hid them under the oak which was by Shechem. And they journeyed: and the terror of God was upon the cities that were round about them; and they did not pursue after the sons of Jacob. So Jacob came to Luz, which is in the land of Canaan, that is Bethel, he and all the people that were with him. And he built there an altar, and called the place El-bethel."

Now in the sixteenth verse of that same chapter you will find that he journeyed from Bethel. In the first verse in the chapter God says, "Arise and go to Bethel, and dwell there." That is plain English that God wanted him to stay there, not only to go and tarry for a night, but to dwell there, to live there; but he went from Bethel. He would not stay at Bethel, for he would not obey the voice of God. Is not that the condition of the church now-a-days, drifting off to religion of forms, instead of staying at Bethel where God dwells? In the same verse it says he journeyed from thence; and Rachel, his beloved wife, died. Affliction came. And I believe one reason why we have so many afflictions and sorrows is because we will not stay at Bethel, where God wants us; we will not dwell there.

The next thing you hear is that his sons have gone to Shechem to look after their sheep. And he says to Joseph one day, "Go to Shechem, and see how your brothers are getting on." Now, of course, this may be imagination; it may not be true; but I can imagine they had gone to Shechem because the idols were buried under the oak tree, and they went there to get them back again. You take your sons to Shechem, and you will find it is a good deal easier to take them down there than it is to get them out; it is a good deal easier to lead them into sin than to deliver them from it. So Jacob sent Joseph down to Shechem; and while he was wandering in the field looking after his brethren, not being able to find them, a stranger came along and said he had heard them say they were going to Dothan; and Joseph went to Dothan, and when his brethren saw him coming, they said, Here comes that dreamer; we will cut his dreams short now; he is going to make us, with our parents, worship and bow down to him.

When Joseph came they had murder in their hearts, and they were going to slay him; but Reuben prevailed against them, and they threw him into a pit; but afterwards he was sold to some Ishmaelites, and taken down to Egypt; and they took off his coat of many colors.

Jacob had the same failing that his father and mother had; he loved Joseph and Benjamin better than any of the rest of his sons, and that caused jealousy; and where there is partiality in the family it always makes trouble; it stirs up the old Adam in most of us. They took the coat of many colors and killed a kid and dipped it in its blood, and took it back again to the old man, saying they were afraid something had happened to Joseph; that they had found this coat in the field, and it looked very much like their brothers. The old man took it and looked at it. You can see the gray-haired old man examine it. Forty or fifty years have passed away since he deceived his aged father, and his boys are coming back with a lie upon their lips. They are deceiving him: and in their hypocrisy they rose up to comfort their father when they knew it was a downright lie; that the boy had not been torn to pieces by the wild beasts, and that in all probability he was alive and well in Egypt. But for twenty long years the old man had to carry his great sorrow and burden. I can see him at night, lying upon his bed, and in his sleep he dreams of poor Joseph torn by the wild beasts; he can hear the piercing cries of that loving son. Twenty long years Jacob had to reap. Ah, it takes us much longer to reap than to sow. Jacob told that lie, and we now see him reaping it; we are not told that he confessed it to his father before he died, or even to Esau. And now we find that he is reaping just what he sowed. And then you will see that when he got to Egypt, if you will turn over to the closing up of his life, he took down there a very strange testimony for that heathen king. I can imagine after he had been in the presence of Pharaoh, and told what a hard journey he had had through life, the king would say, "I don't want that kind of religion."

And these earthly-minded Christians, who are trying to drive hard bargains with the world, and making the most out of this life - they do not win many people, nor have such a prosperous journey after all. It is a good deal better to be right with God, even if we do not make money quite so fast; it is more profitable to have a clear conscience with God, and a mind void of offense, and to be poor in this worlds goods, than to have wealth that has been gathered in the way a great many accumulate their wealth - by working on Sundays, and by defrauding the poor, and grinding the unfortunate. Now, see what Jacob has to say:

"And Jacob said unto Pharaoh, The days of the years of my pilgrimage are a hundred and thirty years; few and evil have the days of the years of my life been, and have not attained unto the days of the years of the life of my fathers in the days of their pilgrimage."

He says, "I have had a stormy voyage of it." Surely such testimony will not win the king of Egypt to the God of the Hebrews. How unlike Daniel, who, by taking a firm stand when he first went to Babylon and doing right, living for the God of Heaven and with the love of God in his soul continually, won that mighty monarch, Nebuchadnezzar, to the God of his people; and if Jacob had been true he might have some sown good seed all through his pilgrimage; and he might have stood before the monarch of Egypt and told him what a blessed journey he had had; how he had been able to serve the God of his fathers, and how the God of his fathers blessed him. But he says, "Few and evil are my days."

If you want to find out whether a man has really been successful, and has had a glorious Christian life and a beautiful voyage through this world, you want to take his whole life, from the cradle, and follow him to his grave. That is the way to study the Bible; not to pick up a chapter here of one who left home with a lie upon his lips; how God met and dealt in grace with him; but you want to see also how God dealt in government with him. God rides in a chariot of two wheels - grace and government - and the two roll side by side. You will find God dealing in grace and government with Jacob. That is the way He deals with all His children.

So let us be careful, and see to it that we are sowing good seed. And if we have told a lie let us confess it, and ask God to take it away - root it out at once. We cannot afford to be deceitful; we cannot afford to rest in shams and profess to be what we are not. God wants honesty. God wants truth in the inward parts.

CHAPTER 11: JOHN THE BAPTIST

THE CONTEMPLATION OF no Bible character quickens me more than the life and character of John the Baptist. I never touch that life but I get a blessing. I used to think that I should liked to have lived in his day, and in the times of some of the prophets; but I have given up that idea long ago: for when a prophet appears, it is when the priests have been unfaithful, religion is at a low ebb, and everything is in disorder and confusion. When John appeared it was as black as midnight. The Old Testament had been sealed up by Malachi's proclamation of the Lord's coming, and of the forerunner who should introduce Him.

With Malachi, prophecy ceased for four hundred years; then John came, preaching repentance and preparing the way for the dispensation of the grace of God. The word John means the grace and mercy of God. He looked back upon the past, and looked forward to the future. I will not dwell upon his birth, although it is interesting to read in Luke 1 the conversation of Gabriel with Zacharias, Johns father, when he was executing the priests office before God, and what took place when John was born. As in the case of Jesus, his name and his birth were announced beforehand. When John was born there was considerable stir but it soon died out. The death of Christ would have died out of men's recollection but for the Holy Ghost.

Notwithstanding the wonders attending Johns birth, for thirty years he dropped out of sight. Many events had taken place during that period. The Roman Emperor had died; Herod, who had sought the lives of the young children when he heard that Jesus was born King of the Jews, was dead; the shepherds were gone: Simeon and Anna, the prophet and prophetess, were gone; the father of John the Baptist was gone; and all the rumors that were afloat at the time of Johns birth had died out and were forgotten, when all at once he burst upon the scene like the flashing of a meteor. There was a voice heard in the wilderness, and the cry came, "Repent: for the kingdom of Heaven is at hand!"

There had been a long line of prophets. He was the last prophet of the Law; he was to close up that dispensation; he stood upon the threshold of the new age, with one foot upon the old and the other upon the new dispensation. He told them what had taken place in the past, and what would take place in the future.

All the Evangelists speak of John. Matthew says, "In those days came John the Baptist preaching in the wilderness of Judea." Mark says, "The voice of one crying in the wilderness, Prepare ye the way of the Lord, make his paths straight." In Luke we read, "The word of God came unto John, the son of Zacharias, in the wilderness." And John, the beloved, says, "There was a man sent from God, whose name was John."

That is the way in which these four men introduce him.

Another thing that stirred the people and moved them was his dress. It was like Elijah's, which was of camels hair, with a leather girdle. His preaching was like that of Elijah. No name could arouse the nation like Elijah's name. And when the news began to spread from town to town, and at last reached Jerusalem, that one had risen like unto Elijah in appearance and dress; that the eloquence of Heaven and the power of God were upon him; that he was a Nazarene from his birth; - when these strange rumors got abroad, the people flocked to hear him. It is remarkable that he never performed one miracle nor gave one sign, and yet he moved the whole nation!

People tell us that they do not believe in revivals. There never was a country moved so suddenly and awakened so quickly as was Judea under the preaching of John and Jesus Christ. Talk about sensational preaching! If by that term you mean preaching designed merely to impress the outward senses, then their preaching was not sensational; but if you mean preaching calculated to produce a striking effect, then it was indeed sensational. The greatest sensation that any nation ever witnessed was brought about by these mighty preachers. Some great patriarchs, prophets and kings - some wonderful men had arisen; but now the Jewish world was about to gaze upon its greatest. It was moved from center to circumference. I am amused to hear some people talk against revivals. If you take up history, you will see that every church has sprung out of revivals. This was the mightiest work the church had seen. It was sudden. It was not long before you could hear the tramp of thousands flocking from the towns into the desert to hear a man who had no commission from his fellow-men; who had gone through no seminary nor college; who had not been brought up in the temple among the sons of Levi; who belonged to no sect or party; who had no D. D., LL. D., or any handle to his name, but simply John; a Heaven-sent man, with a Heaven given name. He had no prestige in Jerusalem, nor any influential committee meetings. He was simply John the Baptist, preaching in the wilderness! And away went the crowd to hear him, and many believed him. Why? Because he was sent from God.

In New York, or London, or any large city, any man of note can gather a large audience; but let him go away into the desert and see if he can draw the inhabitants from the large cities to hear him, as John did. Like Elijah, he was intrepid and uncompromising. He did not preach to please the people for he denounced their sins. When the Pharisees and Sadducees came to his baptism, he cried out, O generation of vipers, who hath warned you to flee from the wrath to come? And to the Jews, who prided themselves on belonging to the seed of Abraham, he said, Think not to say within yourselves, We have Abraham to our father; for I say unto you, that God is able of these stones to raise up children unto Abraham. He tore off the mask of their hypocrisy, warned them against trusting in their self-righteousness, and told them to bring forth fruits meet for repentance. There was no pandering to their prejudices, nor truckling to their tastes or wishes. He delivered his message as he had received it from God; he asked no favors; he talked plainly, and called things by their right names.

We have in Matthew just a glimpse, a specimen, of his courageousness. He brought the law right down upon those who boasted of themselves. "And now," said he, "the ax is laid unto the root of the trees, therefore every tree that bringeth not forth good fruit is hewn down and cast into the fire." And in Luke we read that the people asked him, "What shall we do then?" They had an inquiry-meeting right there!

That is the beginning; but he did not leave them there. You may bring down the law, and cry "Reform! Reform!" "Repent! Repent!" but that leaves a man outside the Kingdom of God; that does not bring him to Christ; and it will not be long before he goes back to his sins. In every one of his sermons John alluded to the coming Messiah.

The bank of the Jordan was his pulpit, the desert his home; when his message was delivered he retired again into the wilderness. His food was locusts and wild honey; there was not a beggar who did not fare better than he. He did not shun to declare the whole counsel of God. He kept back nothing.

We read: "Then went out to him Jerusalem and all Judea, and all the region round about Jordan." Think of the whole population going out into the wilderness to hear this wonderful open-air preacher, to be baptized of him in Jordan, confessing their sins? John was a preacher of repentance. Perhaps no one ever rang out the word Repent like John the Baptist. Day after day, as he came out of the desert and stood on the banks of that famous river, you could hear his voice rolling out, Repent! for the kingdom of Heaven is at hand. We can almost now hear the echoes of his voice as they floated up and down the Jordan. Many wonderful scenes had been witnessed at that stream. Naaman had washed away his leprosy there; Elijah and Elisha had crossed it dryshod; Joshua had led through its channel the mighty host of the redeemed on their journey from Egypt into the promised land, but it had never seen anything like this: men, women, and children, mothers with babes in their arms, Scribes, Pharisees, and Sadducees, publicans and soldiers, flocked from Judea, Samaria, and Galilee, to hear this lonely wilderness prophet.

What excited them most was not his cry, "Repent," nor that they were to be baptized, confessing their sins, in order to the remission of their sins; but it was this, "He that cometh after me is mightier than I." How it must have thrilled the audience when they heard him proclaim! - There is One coming after me; I am only the herald of the coming King. You know that when kings travel in Eastern countries they are preceded by heralds who shout, "The king is coming!" and they clear the highways, repair the bridges, and remove the stumbling blocks. John announced that he was only His fore-runner; and that He himself was nigh at hand. Perhaps at the after-meetings some would inquire, "When is He coming?" "He is coming unexpectedly, suddenly, and we shall see the Spirit of God descending and remaining upon Him. He may be here tomorrow." And as John preached His first coming, so we preach the second coming of Christ. It is always safe, for He said that He was coming again; and none can hinder it. We are told to watch - for death? No; for the second coming of the Lord. At length the time came when John still more mightily moved his hearers by declaring, He is among us. He is in our midst. For four thousand years had the Jews been watching for the event which it was the immediate mission of the Baptist to predict. It had been a long time to be looking into the mists of the future for the Seed of the woman that should bruise the head of the serpent; but the mists had rolled away at last.

One day there came down from Jerusalem a very influential committee, appointed by the chief priests, to ask that wilderness preacher whether he were the Messiah or Elijah, or who or what he was. In John, we read that they made their appearance when he was in the very zenith of his popularity, preaching perhaps to twenty thousand people. Pushing their way up to where he was, they said, "We have been sent to inquire who you are. Are you the long-looked-for Messiah?" What an opportunity he had to pass himself off as the Christ. All were musing as to who he was. Some said that he really was the long-looked-for One. He was one of the grandest characters that ever trod this earth. Instead of elevating, he humbled himself.

The great tendency with men is to make themselves out a little bigger than they are, to make it appear that there is more of them than there really is. Most men, as you get nearer to them, grow smaller and smaller. But John grows larger and larger! Why? Because he is nothing in his own sight. So he replied to the Committee, "Take back word to those who sent you: I am Mr. Nobody. I am a voice to be heard, and not to be seen. I am here to proclaim the coming of Him whose shoe latchet I am not worthy to unloose." That is a grand character! He confessed, I am not the way; I am a finger-post pointing to the way. Walk in it. Do not follow me, but Him that is coming. I have found the way, and have come to herald the glad tidings. I wish all Christian workers would have the spirit of John, and get behind the cross, and be a mere sign-post pointing out Christ. John the Baptist was very little in his own estimation, but the angel had said before his birth, He shall be great in the sight of the Lord. And this was his greatness, that he cried, "Behold the Lamb of God! I am nothing; He is all in all." Let that be our testimony.

"And this is the record of John, when the Jews sent priests and Levites from Jerusalem to ask him, Who art thou? And he confessed, and denied not; but confessed, I am not the Christ. And they asked him, What then? Art thou Elijah? And he saith, I am not. Art thou that prophet? And he answered, No. Then said they unto him, Who art thou? that we may give an answer to them that sent us. What sayest thou of thyself? He said, I am the voice of one crying in the wilderness, Make straight the way of the Lord, as said the prophet Esaias," quoting Scripture; for Isaiah had prophesied that there should be a voice heard in the wilderness, "Prepare ye the way of the Lord."

Do you know what happened the next day? One of the most exciting things that ever took place on this earth. The next day the deputation, who waited upon this desert preacher, had perhaps returned to Jerusalem, or they may have been still on the banks of the Jordan. I think I see the crowds of men and women leaning forward with breathless eagerness to catch every word as it falls from the lips of John. He pauses suddenly in the middle of a sentence, his appearance changes, the eye that has been so keen quails, the bold rugged man shrinks back, and, as he stands silent and amazed, every eye is upon him.

Suppose at some great gathering I should stop preaching for a minute, the congregation would not know what had happened. They would ask, "Has he lost the thread of his discourse? Is sickness stealing over him? Has death laid his icy hand upon him?" But John stops. The people wonder what it means. The eye of the Baptist is fixed; and the crowd gives way before a Man of no very extraordinary mien, who approaches the Jordan, and addressing John, asks to be baptized." Baptize you?" he remonstrates. It was the first man whom he had hesitated to baptize. The people are asking, "What does this mean?" John says, "I have need to be baptized of Thee, and comest Thou to me? I am not worthy to baptize Thee." The Master said, "Suffer it to be so now, for thus it becometh us to fulfill all righteousness;" and they both went down into the Jordan, and Jesus was baptized by John. The Master commanded, and John obeyed. It was simple obedience on his part.

Canon Farrar, in his Life of Christ, thus describes this wonderful scene: "To this preaching, to this baptism, in the thirtieth year of His age, came Jesus from Galilee. John was His kinsman by birth, but the circumstances of their life had entirely separated them. John, as a child, in the house of the blameless priest, his father, had lived at Juttah, in the far south of the tribe of Judah, and not far from Hebron. Jesus had lived in the deep seclusion of the carpenters shop in the valley of Galilee. When He first came to the banks of the Jordan, the great forerunner, according to his own emphatic and twice-repeated testimony, knew Him not. Though Jesus was not yet revealed as the Messiah to His great herald prophet, there was something in His look, something in the sinless beauty of His ways, something in the solemn majesty of His aspect, which at once overawed and captivated the soul of John. To others he was the uncompromising prophet; kings he could confront with rebuke; Pharisees he could unmask with indignation; but before this presence all his lofty bearing falls. As when some unknown dread checks the flight of the eagle, and makes him settle with hushed scream and drooping plumage on the ground, so before the purity of sinless life, the wild prophet of the desert becomes like a submissive and timid child. The battle-brunt which legionaries could not daunt, the lofty manhood before which hierarchs trembled and princes grew pale, resigns itself, submits, adores before moral force which is weak in every external attribute, and armed only in an invisible mail...

"John bowed to the simple, stainless manhood before he had been inspired to recognize the Divine commission. He earnestly tried to forbid the purposes of Jesus. He who had received the confessions of all others now reverently and humbly makes his own: I have need to be baptized of Thee and comest Thou to me? The response contains the second recorded utterance of Jesus, and the first word of His public ministry: 'Suffer it to be so now, for thus it becometh us to fulfill all righteousness.'"

Do you tell me that the immense throng are not moved? Every man is holding his breath. And as they came out of the water, the Spirit descended like a dove and abode upon Him, and the voice of Jehovah, which had been silent on earth for centuries, was heard saying from Heaven, "This is My beloved Son, in whom I am well pleased." From the time of the disobedience of the first Adam, God could not say that He was well pleased in man; but He could say so now. As Jesus came up out of the water, the silence of Heaven was broken: God Himself bore witness that He was well pleased with His beloved Son.

What a day that must have been! You have seen the moon shining in the early morning; but as the sun ascends the moon fades away. So now John fades away. The moons light is borrowed. All it can do is to reflect the light of the sun. That is what John did. He reflected the light of the Sun of Righteousness now that He had risen with healing in His wings. From that day John changes his text. He had preached Repent; but now his text is, "Behold the lamb of God, who taketh away the sins of the world." "Behold the Sin-bearer of the world; God's Son come down into this world to bear away its sin. I am nothing now. He is everything!"

Let us notice the testimony that John bore to Christ. The following was the substance of it:

"He that cometh after me is mightier than I; whose shoes I am not worthy to bear; there standeth one among you whom ye know not; He it is who, coming after me, is preferred before me. He shall baptize with the Holy Ghost and with fire. He is the Judge; His fan is in His hand; and He will thoroughly purge His floor and gather His wheat into the garner; but He will burn up the chaff with unquenchable fire. I knew Him not; but He that sent me to baptize with water, the same said unto me, Upon whom thou shall see the Spirit descending, and remaining on Him, the same is He who baptizeth with the Holy Ghost. And after all the people had been baptized in the Jordan, confessing their sins, He came from Galilee to be baptized by me. But I said, I have need to be baptized of Thee, and comest Thou to me? And He answered me, Suffer it to be so now for thus it becometh us to fulfill all righteousness. Then I suffered Him, and I baptized Him. As He went up out of the water He was praying, and the Heaven was opened, and the Holy Ghost descended in a bodily shape like a dove upon Him, and a voice came from Heaven, which said, 'Thou art my beloved Son in whom I am well pleased.' And I saw and bear record that this is the Son of God."

The next day after Jesus had been baptized, John saw Him coming to him and said, "Behold the Lamb of God, which taketh away the sin of the world." Yesterday He had been baptized in the same river of judgment, where all the people had been baptized, confessing their sins, and today John points Him out as the Sin-bearer. And again, the next day, John was standing with two of his disciples, and, looking upon Jesus as He walked, he said, "Behold the Lamb of God!" He did not need to add the words he used the day before. His disciples knew that the Lamb of God was the antitype of all the sacrifices, from Abel's offering to the lamb laid that morning on the altar of burnt-offering. The two disciples heard him speak; they did not ask him what he meant, but they followed Jesus; went home with Him, and abode with Him that day, and became two of His intimate disciples and friends.

John continued effacing, denying himself, and testifying more and more of Jesus. "I am not the Christ: I am sent before Him. He is the Bridegroom, and I the Bridegrooms friend: I rejoice greatly, because of the Bridegrooms voice. This my joy, therefore, is fulfilled. He must increase, but I must decrease. He cometh from above; He is above all. And what He hath heard in Heaven that He testifieth. But no one receives His testimony. He that hath received His testimony hath set to his seal that God is true. For God hath sent Him, and He speaketh the words of God, for God giveth not the Spirit by measure unto Him. The Father loved the Son, and hath given all things into His hand. He that believeth in the Son hath everlasting life: and he that believeth not the Son shall not see life, but the wrath of God is abiding on him."

Yes: "He that cometh from Heaven is above all." No prophet, priest, nor king, ever lived to compare with Him. Jesus Christ had no peer. We ought to bear this in mind, and never put Him on a level with any other man. When Moses and Elijah appeared on the Mount of Transfiguration, Peter said to Jesus, "Let us make here three tabernacles, one for Thee, and one for Moses, and one for Elijah." But while he yet spoke a bright cloud overshadowed them. And when they had lifted up their eyes, they saw no man save Jesus only. Jesus was left alone to show the superiority of the new dispensation, which was represented by Him, over the old dispensation, represented by Moses and Elijah. God's voice said, "This is my beloved Son; hear ye Him." Christ has no equal. He is above all; He is sent by God; yea, He is God; all things were made by Him; he speaks the words of God; and the Spirit is given to Him without measure.

It was not long, however, before jealousy began to rankle in the breasts of Johns disciples. One of the worst things with which Christian people have to contend is jealousy. It is a most accursed viper, and I would to God that it were cast out of all our hearts. This is one of the devils that needs to be cast out. It were, indeed, well if we all possessed the feeling which animated Moses when Joshua asked him to forbid Eldad and Medad from prophesying in the camp: And Moses said unto him, Enviest thou for my sake? would God that all the Lord's people were prophets, and that the Lord would put his Spirit upon them. If ever there were two men who had reason to be jealous, they were Jonathan and John the Baptist; but the one stripped himself of the robe that was upon him, and gave it to David; and the other, when his disciples sought to arouse Johns jealousy of Him of whom he came to bear witness, on account of the great crowds who flocked to His ministry, answered and said, "A man can receive nothing except it be given him from Heaven. Ye yourselves bear me witness, that I said, I am not the Christ, but that I am sent before Him."

I do not know of anything, in all Scripture, more sublime than that one thing. As if John had said, "My joy is fulfilled. I could not be happier. I am the friend of the Bridegroom. I came to introduce Him. I want all my disciples to follow Him. I must decrease, He must increase."

I once heard Dr. Bonar remark that he could tell whether a Christian were growing. In proportion to his growth in grace he would elevate his Master, talk less of what he was doing, and become smaller and smaller in his own esteem, until, like the morning star, he faded away before the rising sun. Jonathan was willing to decrease, that David might increase; and John the Baptist showed the same spirit of humility.

It took a great deal of grace for a man who, like John, had had such vast crowds following him out of the cities into the wilderness, to listen to his preaching, to declare that his mission was accomplished, and that he must retire into obscurity. He gloried in it. As a friend of the Bridegroom, he rejoiced to hear His voice, and that the stone that smote the image would become a great mountain, and fill the whole earth.

I think that John showed more unselfishness than any man that ever lived. He did not know what selfishness was. If we could analyze our feelings, we should find that self is mixed up with almost everything we do; and that this is the reason why we have so little power as Christians. Oh, that this awful viper may be cast out! If we preached down ourselves and exalted Christ, the world would soon be reached. The world is perishing today for the want of Christ. The church could do without our theories and pet views, but not without Christ; and when her ministers get behind the cross, so that Christ is held up, the people will come flocking to hear the Gospel. Selfishness is one of the greatest hindrances to the cause of Christ. Everyone wants the chief seat in the synagogue. One prides himself that he is pastor of this church, and another of that. Would to God we could get all this out of the way and say, "He must increase, but I must decrease." We cannot do it, however, except we get down at the foot of the cross. Human nature likes to be lifted up; the grace of God alone can humble us.

I have no sympathy with those who think that John lost confidence in his Master. From the earliest times a great difference of opinion has existed among ecclesiastical writers as to the question which John from the prison sent his two disciples to ask of Jesus. The difficulty has been stated thus: "If John the Baptist had recognized in our Lord the Eternal Son of God, the Divine Lamb, and the Heavenly Bridegroom, is it possible to believe that he could, within a few months, question whether Jesus was the Christ; and that he should, with a simple desire for information, have asked, Art Thou He that should come, or do we look for another?"

Some have thought that it was so, and have accounted for Johns declension from his former testimony to Jesus, by supposing that the prophetic gift of the Holy Spirit had departed from him. Others have indignantly refused to believe this, and have eagerly defended John by maintaining that he simply sought by sending them to Jesus to remove the doubts of the disciples themselves. I have strongly urged this view myself in preference to the other, for I cannot believe that this noble man, who was filled with the Holy Ghost from his mothers womb, and who had been his appointed forerunner, became discouraged by a few months in prison, and gave up his confidence in Jesus as the promised Messiah.

I think, however, that Dr. Reynolds, in his Lectures on John the Baptist, has thrown much light on this subject, and has shown that John may quite consistently have sent to ask this question; he says:

"Until the death, resurrection, and ascension of Jesus had taken place, until the descent of the Spirit, Johns prophecies were not completely fulfilled. He may, nay, he must, have had ideas of the Coming One which Jesus had not yet realized. There is nothing, therefore, unworthy of Johns character, nothing incompatible with Johns testimonies, in the supposition that he did not see the whole of his ideal embodied in the ministry of Jesus... There were elements of the Coming One which were clearly a part of that type of Messiah which entered into Johns predictions, and he was specially tempted or moved to ask, Art Thou the coming One, or must we expect another of a different kind from Thyself, to fulfill the larger hope that is throbbing in the heart of Israel?"

After these disciples had left, it was that Christ gave His testimony to John. It was, "Verily I say unto you, Among them that are born of women, there hath not risen a greater than John the Baptist." What a tribute for the Son of God to pay! That must have sounded strange in the ears of the Jews. What! Greater than Abraham the father of the faithful? than Moses, the law-giver? than Elijah and Elisha? than Isaiah, Daniel, and all the prophets? Yes, none in all the world, born of women, greater than John. That is the eulogy which was pronounced on him. Truly he that humbleth himself shall be exalted. John had humbled himself before the Master, and now the Master exalts His faithful servant.

But this testimony of Jesus to His forerunner must not be regarded exclusively or chiefly as relating to his personal character. "There hath not risen a greater prophet than John the Baptist; notwithstanding he that is least in the kingdom of Heaven is greater than he." No prophet under the old dispensation had so great a testimony to bear as John. None before him could say, "There stands among you He that baptizes with the Holy Ghost. Behold the Lamb of God!" But the least disciple in the new dispensation has a still greater testimony. He can declare accomplished salvation: for the essence of the Gospel is Jesus and the resurrection.

John was beheaded for his testimony, the first martyr for the Gospels sake. He sealed his testimony with his blood. He rebuked the king, and told him that it was not lawful for him to live in adultery. He was not ashamed to deliver God's message just as it had been given to him. And no man has lived from the time of John but has enemies, if he be a disciple of Christ. Christ said this, "For John came neither eating nor drinking, and they say, He hath a devil. The Son of man came eating and drinking, and they say, Behold a man gluttonous and a wine bibber, a friend of publicans and sinners."

Think of saying that John the Baptist had a devil! Such a man! That is the worlds estimate. They hated him. Why? Because he rebuked sin. He, the last of a long line of prophets, was beheaded for his testimony, and buried in the land of Moab, just outside the promised land, near to where Moses, the first lawgiver, was buried. His ministry was very short. It lasted only two years. But he had finished his course; he had done his work.

Dear friend, you and I may not have that time to work. Let us consecrate ourselves and get the world and self beneath our feet; and let Christ be all and in all. We must "stoop to conquer." Let us be nothing, and Christ everything. Let the house of Saul wax weaker and weaker, and the house of David wax stronger and stronger. Let us get to the end of self, and adopt as our motto, He must increase, but I must decrease.

AUTHOR	
TITLE	
DATE DUE	BORROWER'S NAME
1758	Jonathan Edwards
1791	John Wesley
1875	Charles Finney
1892	Charles Spurgeon
1898	George Müller
1899	D. L. Moody
1917	Andrew Murray

When finished please return to:

www.ClassicChristianBooks.com

for more
"Great Classics at Great Prices"

Made in the USA
Middletown, DE
25 February 2025

71752092R00044